THE HANDWRITING ON THE WALL

THE HANDWRITING ON THE WALL

SECRETS from the PROPHECIES of DANIEL

Dr. David Jeremiah

WITH C. C. CARLSON

W PUBLISHING GROUP

AN IMPRINT OF THOMAS NELSON

Published in Nashville, Tennessee, by W Publishing, an imprint of Thomas Nelson.

Published in association with Yates & Yates, www.yates2.com.

Thomas Nelson titles may be purchased in bulk for educational, business, fund-raising, or sales promotional use. For information, please e-mail SpecialMarkets@ThomasNelson.com.

Unless otherwise noted, Scripture quotations are taken from the Holy Bible, New International Version®, NIV®. Copyright © 1973, 1978, 1984, 2011 by Biblica, Inc.® Used by permission of Zondervan. All rights reserved worldwide. www.Zondervan.com. The "NIV" and "New International Version" are trademarks registered in the United States Patent and Trademark Office by Biblica, Inc.®

Scripture quotations marked KJV are from the King James Version. Public domain.

Scripture quotations marked TLB are from The Living Bible. Copyright © 1971. Used by permission of Tyndale House Publishers, Inc., Carol Stream, Illinois 60188. All rights reserved.

Any Internet addresses, phone numbers, or company or product information printed in this book are offered as a resource and are not intended in any way to be or to imply an endorsement by Thomas Nelson, nor does Thomas Nelson vouch for the existence, content, or services of these sites, phone numbers, companies, or products beyond the life of this book.

ISBN 978-0-7852-2964-3 (eBook)

Library of Congress Cataloging-in-Publication Data

Jeremiah, David
   The handwriting on the wall: secrets from the prophecies of
Daniel / by David Jeremiah with C.C. Carlson.
      p.   cm.
   ISBN 978-0-7852-2952-0
   1. Bible. O.T. Daniel—Prophecies.   I. Carlson, Carole C.   II. Title.
BS1556.J47   1992
   224'.5015—dc20
92-23120
CIP

Printed in the United States of America

19 20 21 22 23   LSC   10 9 8 7 6 5 4 3 2 1

To the men and women who pray and dream with me each week at the senior staff meeting of Shadow Mountain Community Church

CONTENTS

CONTENTS

PART 3: ISRAEL'S FUTURE

INTRODUCTION

In a questioning age, where are the answers? Where is our world going? Are moral absolutes relevant in our society? Has the arms race ceased and peace in our time become a reality, or is this a historic lull before the storm?

We watch the news and are outraged by another national scandal or international conflict that leaves us reeling like a spaceship out of control. We ask why, oh why, are these things happening?

Many years ago when I began to study the Bible, one of the most intriguing characters I encountered was Daniel. I didn't understand many of his prophecies or whether they were even applicable to my life, but as the events of our day begin to unroll, I realize that his story has such far-reaching significance that we must take him out of the lion's den and discover how his message speaks to our own lives and times.

If we wish to understand today what will happen in the future, we should place the books of Revelation and Daniel between the bookends of our thinking and keep them in perspective as we are involved in these exciting, fateful days.

Daniel's book has a theme of such simplicity that the most brilliant minds in the world have been unable to grasp it. It is just this: God is in charge. No one understood that better than Daniel.

Centuries ago he deciphered some strange signs written by an unseen hand.

Today, more than at any time in history, we should be able to look at our perplexing planet and say that we, too, are able to see the handwriting on the wall.

PART 1

PROLOGUE

1

A PROPHET FOR
OUR TIME

The memo said, "top secret." Every person in the Oval Office had been given orders to arrive promptly at 8 a.m. No one must know, especially CNN, that the president of the United States, the vice president, the Joint Chiefs of Staff, the National Security Council, congressional leaders, and selected members of the cabinet had been called for this executive briefing. The object: to hear a futuristic projection of the rise and fall of our planet's major countries and their leaders. This was not a strategy meeting. This was to be the unveiling of the destiny of the world.

The president never looked more serious. He sat facing his advisers, men and women of keen intelligence whom he had entrusted with decisions that could affect millions of lives. With his fingers pressed together under his chin, he looked like he was praying. Considering the state of the world, his attitude was logical. When he signaled to an armed guard, the door was opened to allow one man to enter. The man hesitated for a moment and glanced at the illustrious gathering of military and political might. The president pointed to a chair directly in front of the polished executive desk. The man took his seat and faced the leadership advisers of the most powerful nation on earth.

The secretary of state cleared his throat. The chairman of the Joint Chiefs wiped his forehead nervously. The secretary of defense looked at his polished shoes. Tension was high.

"Gentlemen," the president said soberly, "you are about to hear the future of the world as we know it. Listen carefully, for your very lives are at stake."

WHO WAS THIS MAN?

Is this an imaginary scenario, or could it happen someday? What is fiction today may easily be fact tomorrow.

This scene did occur in another country with different players. One man, divinely inspired, accurately prophesied the rise and fall of empires and their rulers. Scholars have scoffed and doubters have discredited, but history has substantiated his words and the future will verify his predictions. Believing or disbelieving what this man said could change our lives forever.

Who was this man? Some of his critics say he wrote his book of history and prophecy after the fact. They might compare him to the members of the modern-day Procrastinators Club, who predicted on January 1, 1992, that the Persian Gulf War would be over in 1991, that Gorbachev would topple, and the Soviet Union disintegrate. "We just now got around to our predictions," the president of the club said.

Daniel is the man. Yet no matter how his critics have tried to discredit him or belittle the book that bears his name, they have failed miserably. Their names are forgotten, and his name lives on as a man of intense integrity and profound piety.

We cannot pass him off today as just the man in the lions' den or a dreamer of surrealistic dreams. To know Daniel is to learn how to live today and look at the future with confidence.

This is not merely a biography of someone we should know, but an outline of our future. It's not the images in a crystal ball or the babbling of a clairvoyant, but the truth contained in the Book of books.

DANIEL ON THE WITNESS STAND

The prosecutors of Daniel are the liberal scholars who find he is an embarrassment to them. They level their energy in trying to destroy his credibility. He has been under attack more than the book of Genesis. According to his critics, prophecy is an impossibility. There is no such thing as foretelling events to come; therefore, a book that contains predictions must have been written after the fact. They claim his book is fiction written like prophecy in order that it might be more interesting to the readers.

When the prosecution presents their case before the jury, they use, whether they realize it or not, the conclusions of a man by the name of Porphyry who lived in AD 233. He wrote fifteen books with the revealing title *Against the Christians*. Porphyry became a polytheist, which means he embraced many gods and worshiped them. One of his favorite targets was Daniel. He did everything he could to prove that this book was written about 165 BC, and that all the events the book of Daniel prophesied were written after they had already come to pass.

TESTIMONY OF DANIEL'S CONTEMPORARIES

When Ezekiel takes the witness stand, he is very sure of Daniel's existence and writing, for they were neighbors in Babylon. If the prosecution does not believe Daniel, then they have a problem with Ezekiel also.

> The word of the LORD came to me: "Son of man, if a country sins against me by being unfaithful and I stretch out my hand against it to cut off its food supply and send famine upon it and kill its men and their animals, even if these three men—Noah, Daniel and Job—were in it, they could save only themselves by their righteousness," declares the Sovereign LORD. (Eze. 14:12–14)

If the prosecutors can't deal with Daniel, they will have to call Noah and Job to the witness stand too.

In Ezekiel 28:3, God was speaking to the prince of Tyre, and He said, "Are you wiser than Daniel?" He didn't say Solomon, who is generally named as the wisest man who lived, but He named Daniel, which shows what God thought of him.

TESTIMONY OF THE ARCHAEOLOGISTS

If the prosecution cannot discredit the witness, then they search for contradictions in his testimony. The first and second verses of Daniel say that Nebuchadnezzar, the ruler of Babylon, took vessels from the temple at Jerusalem and brought them into the treasury of his god.

"Never heard of such a thing," says the prosecuting attorney. "That was a completely unknown custom. We can't find any reference in ancient history to such a practice."

Suddenly the archaeologists burst into the room, brushing the dirt from their hands and placing their shovels and sieves in front of the judge. They have discovered an inscription that proves

Nebuchadnezzar always put his choicest spoils into his house of worship. Just one of those peculiar habits of the king.

In the first chapter of Daniel there is reference to a fellow by the name of Ashpenaz, who was master of the eunuchs. The prosecution says, "No one ever heard of this fellow. He was just another fictional character out of Daniel's fantasy."

During the last century, the name Ashpenaz has been found on the monuments of ancient Babylon. It says, "Ashpenaz, master of eunuchs in the time of Nebuchadnezzar."

If the prosecution can trip the defendant on details, he can cast doubt on his credibility. The opponents of the Word of God love to say, "But the Bible contradicts itself."

In the fifth chapter of the book of Daniel, the story is told of Belshazzar, king of Babylon, who is said to have been slain during a drunken feast on the night Babylon fell. Secular history says the king of Babylon at that time was Nabonidus. Who is right? No one knew how to reconcile these two accounts until Sir Henry Rawlinson discovered an inscription on a cylinder found in the Euphrates River. It cleared up the problem. There were two kings of Babylon during Daniel's later life, a father and a son. Nabonidus, who occupied a stronghold outside the city, had his eldest son, Belshazzar, as co-regent. He allowed him to use the royal title. Belshazzar was slain while defending the city; Nabonidus was spared. This detail explains Daniel 5:29, where it says: "Then at Belshazzar's command, Daniel was clothed in purple, a gold chain was placed around his neck, and he was proclaimed the third highest ruler in the kingdom."

Daniel was the third ruler because there were already two others, Nabonidus and Belshazzar. So the prosecutor returns to his seat and searches for more incriminating evidence to indict Daniel.

THE STAR WITNESS

When this Person takes the stand, the prosecution is at a loss. In Matthew 24:15, Jesus said, "So when you see standing in the holy place 'the abomination that causes desolation,' spoken of through the prophet Daniel."

Jesus said that in the Old Testament scriptures, Daniel the prophet wrote about the abomination of desolation. He said Daniel was for real. With that testimony, I know I can go through the book of Daniel and dig out its truth with full confidence that I have God's word in my hands.

The defense rests.

DANIEL'S THEME

When God wants His work to be done, He turns to His children. Jesus said, "Let your light shine before men, that they may see your good deeds and praise your Father in heaven" (Matt. 5:16).

Most of us love praise. We display our trophies, blue ribbons, and awards on the wall. We love the applause of an audience. Nothing wrong with that. But I'm reminded of Corrie ten Boom, who found it difficult to accept all the adulation that came to her after the success of her books and the movie of her life. Then she prayed about it, and "the Lord showed her a beautiful way of using the tributes and accolades: each one would represent a beautiful flower, and then, at night, she would collect them into a beautiful bouquet and give them back to Jesus, saying 'Here, Lord, they belong to you!'"[1]

In the same way, Daniel did not look for personal recognition, although he was intelligent, perceptive, strong, and sensitive. His book reveals much of his character, but the theme is not his greatness;

rather, it is that "the Most High is sovereign over the kingdoms of men and gives them to anyone he wishes" (Dan. 4:25).

The book of Daniel has a high and lofty view of the sovereignty of God. The theme is: there is a God in heaven. The book repeats that He is the great God, He is the God of gods, the King of heaven. When we understand that prevailing theme, we are able to understand how God may use some people for His purposes, even when they are not His own children. For instance, we read in Daniel 1:1–2: "In the third year of the reign of Jehoiakim king of Judah, Nebuchadnezzar king of Babylon came to Jerusalem and besieged it. And the Lord delivered Jehoiakim king of Judah into his hand."

Nebuchadnezzar thought he captured the city. The *Babylonian Daily News* probably headlined, NEBUCHADNEZZAR CONQUERS KING OF JUDAH. No, he didn't. God gave him that victory.

When Daniel interpreted Nebuchadnezzar's dream, he said, "You, O king, are the kings of kings. The God of heaven has given you dominion and power and might and glory" (Dan. 2:37). How did Nebuchadnezzar—a wicked, despotic king—come to the throne of Babylon? It is simple. The God of heaven gave it to him.

Later, Daniel was speaking to Belshazzar and said, "O king, the Most High God gave your father Nebuchadnezzar sovereignty and greatness and glory and splendor" (Dan. 5:18). Sometimes God uses even the worst of men to carry out His will. Later we will meet Cyrus, king of Persia, another corrupt man who was also a tool of God's (see also Isa. 44:28).

Daniel praised the God of heaven and said:

> "Praise be to the name of God for ever and ever;
> wisdom and power are his.
> He changes times and seasons;

he sets up kings and deposes them.
He gives wisdom to the wise
and knowledge to the discerning." (Dan. 2:19–21)

This book is being written during an election year in the United States. Many people will work hard to see that their candidate is elected to a local, state, or national office. If he or she is elected, they may have a victory celebration and shout, "We did it! We won!" They didn't win. God put that person in office. I don't always understand how God does it, but I know that He rules in the halls of government today, just as He has done in the past and will do in the future.

What Daniel will teach us, if we allow him, is that the kingdoms of this world are passing away and the kingdom of heaven is coming to pass. As I see this old world reeling and rocking on its axis, I am more motivated than ever to proclaim what God has prophesied, especially through His prophet, Daniel.

Christians should be the calmest people on earth. We have no right to run around this world in frenzied activity, staying up and walking the floor at night, wondering what is going to happen. God in heaven rules the kingdoms of men.

ABOVE THE CROWD

Daniel came to Babylon as a teenager and stayed until he was past eighty. Through all those years of captivity, he was a leading official in three kingdoms. As he walked the halls of the palaces, he could watch how God worked in the lives of kings.

Daniel was there to see the ruthless Nebuchadnezzar at work. This man possessed the cumulative cruelty of Napoleon, Mussolini, Hitler, Stalin, and Hussein. He was a dictator of the first order. We get a clue about him when we read, "all the peoples and nations and men of every language dreaded and feared him. Those the king wanted to put to death, he put to death; those he wanted to spare, he spared" (Dan. 5:19). This was a man who put away those he didn't like and promoted those he liked. He ruled his kingdom on the basis of whim.

One man did not fear him, and he watched as God brought the king to his knees, literally and figuratively.

Daniel was also there to see Belshazzar "set [himself] up against the Lord of heaven" (Dan. 5:23). He was presumptuous enough to compare himself to God. One night God sent him a message. That message is one we can hear today, echoing through the centuries to our modern world.

Daniel watched God deal with Darius the Mede and Cyrus the Persian. Daniel was the man behind the scenes watching God at work in the halls of the leaders of nations.

During all the troubles of the nation, from the king's insanity to the murder of his successors, the whirling intrigues, the plots and persecutions, Daniel stood like an iron pillar in a hurricane because the sovereign God of the universe was also the sovereign God of his life.

DANIEL TODAY

If Daniel were sitting in the Oval Office today, he would look at many faces that were openly hostile. Most of the men and women assembled there would be graduates of prestigious universities with many years in private and public service. Some would have been strategists in several wars; others would be the heads of large corporations. What could they learn from someone who lived in a country that no longer exists?

However, a few might edge forward in their chairs, eager to hear and understand what this prophet had to say. They would be the ones who believe his credentials.

The president would break the tension. "We are here to find out what Daniel has to say about the future of the world as we know it. I, for one, have found his book fascinating—but baffling. I propose, ladies and gentlemen, that we hear him out with open minds."

2

HISTORY IN A CAPSULE

Graveyards and wasted lives are tragic results of warnings that were scorned or ignored. Why don't we listen? When the yellow light is flashing, the red light follows. When God gives His inspired prophets strong admonitions for His people, it's time to take notice. Wake up.

In Daniel 1:1–2, we read: "In the third year of the reign of Jehoiakim king of Judah, Nebuchadnezzar king of Babylon came to Jerusalem and besieged it. And the LORD delivered Jehoiakim king of Judah into his hand, along with some of the articles from the temple of God. These he carried off to the temple of his god in Babylonia and put in the treasure house of his god."

Did the collapse of Judah and the capture of its king come as a surprise? For many years the threat of judgment hung over that country. God had warned them, and they would not listen. In fact, their attitude toward God was like that of the people in Noah's day. They were having a wild time, right up until the moment Noah and his entourage entered the ark. It was too late to repent when they were going under for the last time. That's the way it was in Judah when the prophets were speaking and the people had their eyes and ears closed. Live it up. Have another drink.

GOD SAYS, "ENOUGH IS ENOUGH"

One day God had His fill. He had extended His mercy for generations, and He said in His heart, *I won't put up with this anymore.*

I don't presume to put words in the mouth of the Lord, but the consequences were obvious. Habakkuk the prophet had a vivid prediction of the coming Babylonian invasion of Judah. He lived in Judah and was deeply concerned about the wickedness of his native land. He complained that God seemed to be doing nothing. The prophet was much like some people in America today who say, "Why doesn't God stop all of this crime and immorality?" This is a basic theme heard throughout the ages: why does evil go unpunished?

God answered Habakkuk:

> Look at the nations and watch—
> and be utterly amazed.
> For I am going to do something in your days
> that you would not believe,
> even if you were told.
> I am raising up the Babylonians,
> that ruthless and impetuous people,
> who sweep across the whole earth
> to seize dwelling places not their own. (Hab. 1:5–6)

This was the nation that would punish Judah. What an astonishing historical event! The Babylonian Empire seemed to spring up overnight. It was like a meteor that streaked across the night sky without warning. God used Babylon to bring judgment upon His people for seventy years. At the end of that time, the Babylonian Empire died just as quickly as it had come into existence.

It's not unthinkable that the same scenario could happen to us. When we read the book of Habakkuk, we find that the prophet wrestled with the question, "How could God use such a wicked nation to punish His own people?" But God did it with Assyria. God did it with Babylon. And if God chooses to do it, He will do it with America unless we get on our knees, repent before Him, and pray for a revival in our country.

Strong words are needed today, just as they were in the time of the prophets.

DOUBLE-CROSS

On the throne in Jerusalem at the time of the Babylonian invasion was a wicked man named Jehoiakim. His wickedness was unusual because he was born into the family of Josiah, a godly king. Jehoiakim was a rotten apple on a beautiful family tree; he had lived through the great revival under the reign of Josiah, but it didn't touch him.

While Jehoiakim was on the throne in Judah, Nebuchadnezzar laid siege to the city of Jerusalem, but he left Jehoiakim in charge after the Babylonian conquest. However, Jehoiakim heard that the Egyptians were in the area, and he decided to form an alliance with them and put down old Nebuchadnezzar.

Enter Jeremiah, known as the weeping prophet, who went to King Jehoiakim and said, "Look, king, don't do that. You are under judgment and Babylon is your leader right now. Don't make any alliances with Egypt."

Jehoiakim wouldn't listen. In fact, he became so angry with

Jeremiah for preaching that message that one day he said, "I've had enough of you, old man. You're going to prison."

Jeremiah was carted off to jail, but the king underestimated him. One day the prophet called for a secretary, a man by the name of Baruch, to come to his cell. Jeremiah said, "I have some dictation for you." The scribe whipped out his scroll and copied the same prophecy Jeremiah had been preaching in the temple and in front of Jehoiakim. Then he said, "Baruch, take this and read it to the people in the temple."

Word traveled fast, and soon Jehoiakim heard about this audacious act. He was sitting in his palace, warming himself in front of a roaring fire, when one of his court officials brought in the scroll and read it to him. The king didn't like what Jeremiah said at all, so he took out his penknife, cut the scroll to shreds, and threw it in the fire.

This is one of the most fearful passages I've ever read. Here was a man who claimed to be a man of God, and yet he destroyed the Word of God. But the Lord dealt with Jehoiakim. The Scripture says:

> Therefore, this is what the LORD says about Jehoiakim king of Judah: He will have no one to sit on the throne of David; his body will be thrown out and exposed to the heat by day and the frost by night. I will punish him and his children and his attendants for their wickedness; I will bring on them and those living in Jerusalem and the people of Judah every disaster I pronounced against them, because they have not listened. (Jer. 36:30–31)

In the pulpits of our land today there are those who claim to be people of God, yet who take this Book and, with the penknife of higher criticism, chop it up and throw what they don't like into the trash. If there are portions of the Scriptures they can't believe because they are supernatural, they ignore or ridicule them. They come before their congregations with a milquetoast Bible that has no power. The Scripture says there will be a Nebuchadnezzar who will topple these men from their pulpits.

I would rather stand before God and face any kind of judgment than have to answer to Him for cutting up His Word and not preaching the inerrant, authoritative, inspired Word of God.

I remember when the president of one of our largest seminaries told the Congress on the Bible that the Bible was not inspired. You could believe some of it, he said, but you didn't have to believe all of it. Out of this seminary come young men and women who become pastors, teachers, and counselors in our churches. They spread the Poor News into our villages and cities.

It might be wise for them to read of Jehoiakim's fate!

When Nebuchadnezzar had Jerusalem surrounded and under his control, he received a special-delivery message from Babylon that his father had died. Since he had to return home, he left Jehoiakim on the throne in Jerusalem, because he knew he was a worthless fellow who would never cause him any problems. To assure the loyalty of the people of Judah, he took some hostages with him to Babylon. He chose about seventy young men and women, with Daniel being one of the hostages. He also tossed in some of the holy things from the temple. Later on we find out how those sacred utensils of worship were used in a drunken orgy.

GIVE US YOUR BRIGHTEST YOUTHS

In pre-World War II Paris, the artists, intellectuals, and bohemian philosophers used to gather on the Left Bank and exchange their ideas on life and destiny. Today, from Harvard to modern Budapest, the bright young people of this generation debate the existence of God and the meaning of the human soul. Their schooling and companions mold their thinking at a time when their minds are inquisitive and searching. The most important thing is to be open-minded, not to be dogmatic in one's opinions.

Allan Bloom, who was a brilliant professor at the University of Chicago, described the prevalent thinking among American university students. He wrote:

> There is one thing a professor can be absolutely certain of: almost every student entering the university believes, or says he believes, that truth is relative. . . . Relativism is necessary to open-mindedness; and this is the virtue, the only virtue, which all primary education for more than fifty years has dedicated itself to inculcating. Openness—and the relativism that makes it the only plausible stance in the face of various claims to truth and various ways of life and kinds of human beings—is the great insight of our times. The true believer is the real danger. . . . The point is not to correct the mistakes and really be right; rather it is not to think you are right at all.[1]

Mind control begins with the young. By destroying their beliefs and indoctrinating them into a counterculture, the ruling forces of evil can capture a generation for their purposes. Today our children are being subverted in a more subtle fashion than the Hitler Youth, but the web of control is just as strong.

Nebuchadnezzar understood the battle for the minds of the young. When he decided to bring back hostages from Judah, he established some exact criteria. He ordered his chief official, Ashpenaz, to choose the scholars with a 4.0 grade point average, the young men who were the sharpest in looks and ability. They were probably between the ages of fourteen and seventeen, mature enough to leave home, but young enough to be reeducated. Daniel was probably about fourteen.

"Ashpenaz, bring me top-notch young people," was the command from the king. "I only want strong, good-looking people around me." (Doesn't that sound like the Hitlerian concept of the master race?) He wanted the best of the best. They were to be "well informed, quick to understand" (Dan. 1:4). Nebuchadnezzar wanted to be sure they had already amassed a lot of information.

Boys like that would be an asset to any parent. Can you imagine the anguish in Jerusalem as seventy of the most outstanding boys were herded off to a foreign country? I have two sons, and I know my own heart would break if they were taken as prisoners of war (POWs).

In our society, as in Babylon, good looks and brains seem to indicate you have it made. It's too bad the people of the world haven't been tuned in to the fact that God sees more in us than those two dimensions.

Daniel and his fellow prisoners also had to be "qualified to serve in the king's palace" (Dan. 1:4). This means they needed to have social graces and the sense to do the right thing. I don't think I would have qualified for that. Growing up in a preacher's home, we didn't have fancy parties or attend society events. I'm sure if I ever met royalty I wouldn't know whether to bow or shake hands. But these young men were to be trained not only in palace protocol but also to learn the Chaldean language and all the knowledge of Babylon in three years. This would be like a crash course at Harvard, MIT, Cal Tech, and Oxford in thirty-six months!

Babylon was the learning center of the world in that day; the curricula for those Hebrew children would have included all the humanistic teaching of the time. The Chaldeans had the reputation of being the wisest men in the world.

CAMPAIGN FOR SEDUCTION

The king's intention was not just to educate these young men, but to brainwash them. He wanted them to look like Jews on the outside but be Babylonian on the inside. This is the aim of most secular universities if the professors do not know Christ; they don't care if you look like a Christian on the outside, attending church or marking a denominational choice on your college application, as long as they can teach you to think like a humanist on the inside.

The cunning strategy of the king was to offer them food and wine worthy of the royal household. He wanted them to be so accustomed to the good life that they would never be tempted to return to their old ways. He wanted them to be obligated to him. Another brainwashing tactic.

In addition to this sense of obligation, the king had another tactic—consolidation. The Scripture says that four Jewish boys had godly names: Daniel meant "God is my judge," Hananiah meant "Jehovah is gracious," Mishael meant "who is like God?," and Azariah meant "Jehovah is my helper." But Nebuchadnezzar changed their names. Daniel became Belteshazzar, meaning "Bel, protect his life;" Hananiah was renamed Shadrach, which means "command of the moon god, Aku;" Mishael was to be Meshach, named after the god Aku; and Azariah was changed to Abednego, a way to honor the second greatest Babylonian god, Nebo. What cunning strategy! Try to get them to forget their homes, their lifestyle, and everything about their godly Jewish heritage.

We don't know how many of those seventy-some youths succumbed to the seduction of Babylon, but one fourteen-year-old said no. He drew the line when it came to the royal food and wine. First of all, none of it was kosher; according to his dietary laws, it was unclean. He also knew that in Babylon, the meat and drink were first offered to the gods of the land before they were brought to the table. Daniel was taking his life in his hands when he refused these gourmet meals.

When God gives us a hard thing to do, there are many reasons not to do it. We can construct all sorts of rationale. Satan has the lists made up for us to follow.

Daniel could have thought, *Wait a minute, I'm just a kid. Why should I be expected to turn down the good life?* Or he could have said, "Look at all of those other fellows. Why should just four of us be denied the king's meat and wine? After all, everybody else is living it up!"

Daniel could have said, "I'm away from home, and Mom and Dad will never know." Someone said that the test of true character is what you do when you know absolutely nobody will find out. Daniel also knew that if he disobeyed, he might not be around very long—Nebuchadnezzar had a reputation for throwing people into the furnace. It was one of his favorite indoor sports. In fact, Jeremiah told about a time when Nebuchadnezzar decided he didn't like someone and had him slowly roasted in the fire while others watched.

Here's the best excuse of all. Daniel could have reasoned, *Now, Lord, I know this isn't exactly right, and I probably shouldn't do this, but I really want a place of leadership in the kingdom, and I know You could really use me if I were your representative to Nebuchadnezzar.* Isn't that spiritual? However, Daniel had learned that it is never right to do wrong in order to do right.

Daniel didn't make a fuss when his name was changed, nor when they wanted him to go to Babylon University, but when they tried to feed him the king's meat, he refused. Why?

In the Old Testament there is no prohibition against taking another name. There is no command against learning what other people have to teach. Moses and Joseph were both assimilated into other cultures. However, in the Bible there is strong prohibition against eating that which has been offered to idols. Where God said no, Daniel said no.

Sometimes Christians argue over the things where God hasn't spoken, while allowing the things He has spoken to slip under the rug. There are certain things God says are wrong. Immorality is wrong. Adultery is wrong. Homosexuality is wrong. Fornication is wrong. God draws the line on what our sexually stimulated society is offering today. If we want the blessing of God upon our lives, we better have the courage and authority to stand as Daniel stood and say, "I will not defile myself, because God has said no."

The same strength that armed Daniel to be a tough-minded teenager and a man of courage is available to us. The marvelous thing is how God blesses when a person is committed. Daniel was not a second-rate believer, obeying God when he felt like it or when it was convenient. As a result, he was blessed in some incredible ways.

3

TRAINING OF A CHAMPION

A young Native American boy living near Prague, Oklahoma, dreamed of becoming a professional football player. When the other boys were playing in the fields, he was running and kicking balls. Practicing long hours, committed to developing his strength and skills, he eventually got his opportunity to play football at the Carlisle Indian Industrial School in Carlisle, Pennsylvania, scoring 25 touchdowns and 198 points in one season and setting a record that was held for years. He became a star baseball player for the New York Giants and won both the decathlon and pentathlon gold medals at the 1912 Olympics in Sweden. In 1950, Wa-Tho-Huk—whose christened name was Jacobus Franciscus Thorpe—changed his name to Jim Thorpe. He was voted the best athlete of the first half of the century. More than fifty years later, when people talk about the greatest athlete of all time, they still mention Jim Thorpe.

Champions are not usually self-trained. Someone sees their potential and works to help them become equipped for the competition. When we applaud an Academy Award winner, we may not know the name of the actor's drama teacher. The coach of the Olympic gold medal winner is forgotten. Who knows the person God used to lead Billy Graham to Christ? But there is a coach for every star.

God Himself had been preparing Daniel for the trials he would face. It was no accident that he was one of the four youths to serve in the king's court. God's training of a man or woman is a thing of wonder. He is always more concerned about the person He is training than He is about the work His student will do. We are in awe of what a person does, like an art student gazing at a Rembrandt painting, but God is excited about who a person is.

BEFORE THE BOOK BEGINS

Daniel grew up during one of the greatest revivals in the history of the southern kingdom of Judah. The king was Josiah, the first good man to sit on the throne in fifty-seven years. (Aren't we blessed to have an election every four years, even if it does turn into a media circus?)

Josiah came to the throne when he was only eight years old. When he was a teenager he began to seek after God. When he had been ruling for twelve years, he brought about some radical reforms. Judah had become a land of false idols; the God of Abraham, Isaac, and Jacob had been replaced with the worship of heathen gods. Josiah was so convicted about the terrible condition of Solomon's temple that he brought in some master builders to restore it to its former glory.

The Scripture says that while the workers were refurbishing the temple, they came upon a very important book: the Book of the Law. Imagine the astonishment of those workers when they uncovered the most valuable document of the Hebrew people. These were the commandments and covenants that the Lord had given to Moses. When Moses went up Mount Sinai, almost eight hundred years before Josiah was king of Judah, the Lord had given him the Ten Commandments and all the laws for His people to follow. Moses read them to the people, and they piously responded, "We will do everything the LORD has said; we will obey" (Ex. 24:7). And yet the book of the covenant, dusty and covered with spider webs, lay lost and neglected in an unused temple.

When Josiah found out about the discovery and heard the words of the Law, he tore his robes. He was completely distraught, and I can understand why (see 2 Chron. 34).

Nothing has changed today. There are men and women across this land who go to church every Sunday and never open their Bibles. In fact, there are churches where the only Bible is the one that sits so impressively on the pulpit and has gathered dust on its opened pages. When we attend a church where people bring their Bibles, we know the Book of the Law has not been lost.

Josiah didn't remain despondent for long. He called a national press conference, and the Bible says everyone from the "least to the greatest" came and heard the king read all of the words of the Book of the Covenant. If anyone came to my church and heard a sermon that long, the sanctuary would be empty after an hour. But the people listened. When he had finished, the king was the first to respond with conviction. It would have been like the president of the United States appearing on every television station and making a public vow to follow the Word of God in all his decision making.

"The king stood by the pillar and renewed the covenant in the presence of the LORD—to follow the LORD and keep his commands, regulations and decrees with all his heart and all his soul" (2 Kings 23:3). What followed was what many of us are praying for in America: a great revival. Judah had never seen anything like the revival that came at the time when Josiah was on the throne and Jeremiah was in the pulpit. It brought the people to their knees.

Unfortunately, Josiah's heirs—Jehoahaz, Jehoiakim, Zedekiah, and a grandson by the name of Jehoiachin—were a nasty lot. If you looked at Josiah, you might say, "The revival was a failure. Why didn't it affect your own family?" However, the period of his reign did touch the lives of Daniel and three of his friends.

God had been preparing Daniel for the moment when he would not be in a safe, comfortable environment, when he was all alone and being tested to take a stand. And one verse in his book is the key to his usefulness for the Lord's work. "But Daniel resolved not to defile himself with the royal food and wine, and he asked the chief official for permission not to defile himself this way" (Dan. 1:8). He said, "No, I can't do that. I will not do what God forbids me to do." He knew the Book of the Law, and he would not violate the Word of God.

If Daniel had not said no to Ashpenaz when the temptation came to him, his history would not have been written in the hall of fame, but in the hall of failure. Everything that follows in this book hinges upon the fact that Daniel purposed in his heart to do what was right.

LITTLE DECISIONS AND BIG CONSEQUENCES

At a single moment in time we may make a decision that affects our entire life. All of us have had those experiences. Take a job. Move to another city. Ask her to marry you. Accept Christ as your Savior. Big decisions are the result of a series of little decisions. I found a bit of advice a father gave to his son when he was about to go out into the world. Written in 1887 by Horatio Richard Palmer, this song is something I would like to claim for my sons and grandsons.

You're starting, my boy, on life's journey,
Along the grand highway of life;
You'll meet with a thousand temptations.
Each city with evil is rife.
This world is a stage of excitement,
There's danger wherever you go;
But if you are tempted to weakness,
Have courage, my boy, to say No!

In courage, my boy, alone lies your safety,
When you the long journey begin,
Your trust in a heavenly Father,
Will keep you unspotted from sin.
Temptations will go on increasing,
As streams from a rivulet flow;
But if you'd be true to your manhood,
Have courage, my boy, to say No!

Be careful in choosing companions,
Seek only the brave and the true,
And stand by your friends when in trial,
Ne'er changing the old for the new;
And when by false friends you are tempted
The taste of the wine cup to know,
With firmness, with patience and kindness,
Have courage, my boy, to say No![1]

It takes guts to say no—whether it was twenty-six hundred years ago or last night, it makes no difference. The resolution of Daniel is a reminder to us, whether it be in the political realm or the church or business or personal life, that we need not bend the rules to be blessed of God. Success is not dependent upon our compromise. Everywhere you see a compromise struck in the Bible you also see a loss.

- Adam compromised God's law and fell right in with his wife's sin. He lost paradise.
- Abraham compromised the truth and lied about Sarah. He almost lost his wife.
- Sarah compromised God's Word and sent Abraham to her servant, Hagar, who bore Ishmael. We lost peace in the Middle East.
- Esau compromised for a meal with Jacob. He lost his birthright.
- Aaron compromised his convictions about idolatry. He lost the privilege of seeing the Promised Land.
- Samson compromised righteous devotion as a Nazarite. He lost his hair, his strength, his eyes, and his life.
- David compromised the moral standard of God and committed adultery with Bathsheba and murdered Uriah. He lost his child.
- Solomon compromised his convictions and married foreign wives. He lost the united kingdom.
- Ahab compromised and married Jezebel. He lost his throne.
- Ananias and Sapphira compromised their word about giving. They lost their lives.
- Judas compromised his supposed love for Christ for thirty pieces of silver. He lost his eternal soul.

Is it any different today? The message of our culture is that if you want to get ahead, you're going to have to break a few rules to do it. I believe we are hungry in our world today for a few men who will stand up and say, "As Daniel was, so will I be."

The story is told about some young people who walked into a high school class that was taught by a godless professor. In one of his lectures he said, "Will all of you who believe the myths of the Bible please stand." Several stood.

Then he added, "Now this semester I am going to free you from this religious Bible nonsense. I have read the Bible, and it is certainly written by a bunch of mixed-up men."

One young Daniel stood up and said, "Sir, the Bible is God's letter to Christians, and if you are confused it's because you're reading somebody else's mail."

GOD'S REFUGE

I don't know what happened to the student and the professor, but I do know that God will take care of the person who refuses to compromise. In Daniel 1:9, right next to the record of Daniel's commitment, it says, "Now God." You can lay out the worst scenario you can imagine, but after that you're in good shape if God takes over.

God gave Daniel favor with the people who counted. When Daniel needed to have his diet approved, he had a friend to help him. But Daniel used good judgment by offering an alternative to the menu. Instead of rebelling, he said, "Look, give me and my three friends a vegetarian diet and at the end of ten days compare how we look with the others who have had the gourmet food from the king's chef." Sounded like a reasonable idea.

God gave Daniel wisdom, just as He will us if we are in His will. If Daniel were to be a speaker in our churches, colleges, and high schools across the nation today, he would say, "I would rather be a captive in Babylon in the will of God, than to be free in Jerusalem out of the will of God."

When we are out of God's will, we're on our own. When we stay where God wants us and do what He wants us to do, then He is committed to take care of us and give us strength. Proverbs 16:7 says, "When a man's ways are pleasing to the LORD, he makes even his enemies live at peace with him."

RESULTS OF AN UNCOMPROMISING LIFE

During an election year we often hear of men or women who are skilled in the art of compromise. Someone said that a compromise is the art of dividing a cake in such a way that everybody believes he got the biggest piece.

An uncompromising life results in courage. When we take the first stand and draw the line, it is like firing the furnace of our own intestinal fortitude. The next step, then, is not so hard. For young people going away to school, the time to take a stand for what is right is on the first day in a new environment. Daniel exhibited that kind of courage when he said, "Thank you for the invitation to eat at the king's table, but I have chosen not to defile myself with that food." He was laying his neck on the chopping block.

Daniel may have heard the story of Zedekiah, one of Josiah's sons in Jerusalem, who tried to escape when he thought Nebuchadnezzar was going to take control of the city. He was caught by the Babylonian king's soldiers. Quickly the order was given for all Zedekiah's children and all the nobles of his inner circle to line up in front of the fugitive king. Then the soldiers went along the line and methodically killed every one of them in front of him. They finished their grisly task by taking a hot sword and putting out his eyes, so that the last thing Zedekiah saw was the vicious execution of his family and friends (Jer. 52:10–11). That was the kind of person Nebuchadnezzar was.

Did it take courage for Daniel to say no to Nebuchadnezzar?

Some of us could take a lesson in courtesy from Daniel. Pounding on the pulpit and calling down fire and judgment on everybody who doesn't agree with us has been an accusation leveled at fighting fundamentalists. But Daniel "asked for permission" and didn't get nasty about it. It has been said that prudence, politeness, and pluck are a fine trio. Instead of defying authority, Daniel made a dignified request.

We can be calm when we are in the will of God and doing what is right. We don't need to be like the preacher who said that when he thought he had a weak point in his sermon, he would shout and bang on the wood. There is a kind of quiet power that comes into our lives if we walk in the power of the Holy Spirit.

Daniel not only had courtesy, he also had confidence. He believed so much in the word of God that he knew God could not possibly let him down. So with assurance, he would have said, "If God be for us, who can be against us?" Holy living always brings confidence. If we are always looking over our shoulders, wondering who is watching or if we'll get caught, perhaps we're not living right. Daniel was living such a holy and righteous life, walking in the power that God had given him, that he wasn't afraid to test his commitment before the whole kingdom.

A CONSISTENT LIFE

Most of us have our good moments, and we love to bask in those times. But it's hard to be consistent day after day. Daniel lived a holy, righteous, godly life in the Babylonian palace for more than seventy years. The last verse in Daniel 1 is a lesson in itself: "And Daniel remained there until the first year of King Cyrus" (Dan. 1:21). Daniel remained in Babylon all through his captivity.

Nebuchadnezzar came and went. Belshazzar came and went. Darius. Cyrus. But Daniel was still there, consistently God's man in the place of influence.

From his youth up he was in the court in a culture that was utterly pagan. And yet he is one of only a few men in the Old Testament about whom we have no report of wrongdoing. In fact, his enemies tried to find a weak link in his character so they could expose him in the *Babylon Enquirer*:

> At this, the administrators and the satraps tried to find grounds for charges against Daniel in his conduct of government affairs, but they were unable to do so. They could find no corruption in him, because he was trustworthy and neither corrupt nor negligent. Finally these men said, "We will never find any basis for charges against this man Daniel unless it has something to do with the law of his God." (Dan. 6:4–5)

The only way they thought they could trip Daniel up was to get into his religion. They had scrutinized him for decades and couldn't find a bad thing to say about him.

It is a sobering thought that we can be good for a long time and then blow it all in a single moment. I have known of men and women in positions of influence who have ruined their lives with one indiscretion or bad decision that caused their reputation to collapse overnight. Solomon was the wisest man who ever lived, but in his old age he corrupted his conviction and died a broken, defeated man.

Daniel, however, was consistent, even though he was a politician of the highest order. If he had followed in the downward spiral of some of our political figures today, we would never have had the prophetic truth he has given us.

REWARDS OF AN UNCOMPROMISING LIFE

We are told today that if we are going to get ahead, we need to bend a few rules, pad some expense accounts, and look out for ourselves. But in the first chapter of Daniel we see a story that contrasts sharply with the world's system of ethics. As a result, God rewarded Daniel in his lifetime. I personally believe that God is still in the business of doing that today. One of the reasons why we have so many problems in our lives as Christians is because we are trying to keep one foot on this side of the street and the other on the opposite side.

What would happen if we would commit ourselves and say, "No matter what it costs, no matter what people say, where God's word draws the line, that's where I'm drawing the line." Someone like that is a champion. It doesn't make any difference what the competition does, or how the others play the game, a person who is sold out to the Lord will always be a winner.

God rewarded Daniel by giving his life a *special impact*. There could be no doubt when he walked into the room after ten days of eating vegetables that Daniel and his friends looked terrific. "At the end of the ten days they looked healthier and better nourished than any of the young men who ate the royal food. So the guard took away their choice food and the wine they were to drink and gave them vegetables instead" (Dan. 1:15–16).

Vegetarians are undoubtedly cheering at this point. But the King James Version calls the food "pulse," which could be a form of cereal. Imagine what the manufacturers of cereal could do with Daniel endorsing their products on television.

It wasn't the food that did it for the Hebrew boys; it was their resolve to do what was right. Psalm 25:14 says, "The secret of the LORD is with them that fear him" (KJV).

God also gave Daniel *special insight*. He could understand

visions and dreams, which is the fulcrum upon which the whole book rests. Daniel's interpretation of visions and dreams spreads through all the ages and into the future. He will go down in history as a man used of God in advance of the major epics of history to point out everything of major consequence that would happen from his time until the reign of Christ.

God also gave Daniel *special influence*. He became influential not only in the court, but also with his companions. Can you image what it was like for Hananiah, Mishael, and Azariah (the true Hebrew names of the three friends) to be close to Daniel? The impact of his life spread to the captives in Babylon. He was the only consistent thing they had throughout the captivity. Ezekiel was there part of the time, but Daniel was "our man in the palace" to the POWs.

I cannot think of anyone else in the entire realm of history who lived his whole life, from teenager to senior citizen, as a constant testimony for God. It all started back on that first day when he was tempted to compromise what he knew was right.

Lord, where are the Daniels today? Or have we come so far into Compromise Country that there is no way out?

PART 2

DESTINY OF NATIONS

4

NIGHT DREAMS AND
DAY VISIONS

I f I insisted that you hear my fascinating account of last night's dream, you might listen with feigned interest but secretly think, *So what?* Dreams are only significant to the dreamer or the psychoanalyst. It has only been within the past hundred years that dreams have been scrutinized carefully. Sigmund Freud began the first comprehensive study of dreams, giving rise to a whole field of psychoanalysis.

In the Bible, God often spoke to His own through dreams and visions. Dreams when they were asleep, visions when awake. "When a prophet of the LORD is among you, I reveal myself to him in visions, I speak to him in dreams" (Num. 12:6). He appeared to Solomon in a dream and told him he could ask for whatever he wanted. In Genesis we hear about Joseph's interpretation of dreams. Jacob dreamed about a stairway between earth and heaven, with angels walking up and down.

God did not limit His speaking through dreams to His children, He also spoke to the pagans. But of all the dreams recorded in the Bible, there is one that is the most amazing of all. It was not given to some pious preacher, but to the vilest world ruler at that time. It was like God revealing to Hitler what was going to happen with the Berlin Wall, the demise of the USSR, and the Second Coming.

BURDEN OF A GUILTY CONSCIENCE

"In the second year of his reign, Nebuchadnezzar had dreams; his mind was troubled and he could not sleep" (Dan. 2:1).

Daniel and his friends had been going to Babylon University for three years. Since Nebuchadnezzar had enrolled them in college, we have to understand that according to Babylonian reckoning, a king did not count his first year as a part of his reign. We have, then, the right time sequence, since it was the second year of his reign, but actually three years had transpired. This may be a small detail, but it is just this type of thinking that adds fuel to the critics who say the Bible is contradictory.

Here was a man who was ruler of the world, secure on his throne, with all of his enemies subdued or in captivity. But he had a royal case of insomnia. In *Hamlet*, Shakespeare wrote, "Conscience does make cowards of us all." For a person with no conscience, such as Nebuchadnezzar, one would think he would sleep like a cat on a soft pillow. But no, his busy brain wouldn't be still. He tossed and turned in the royal bedchamber, and when he finally fell asleep, he had a bizarre dream.

When he awakened, the king bellowed out orders to his staff. "Bring in all of the magicians. Call those guys who write the astrological forecasts in the *Babylonian News*. Bring on the witches and warlocks. And hurry up or I'll have your heads on a platter."

We can imagine that the stargazing crowd broke all records

getting to the palace. They had seen the victims of the king's wrath, and it wasn't a pretty picture.

Nebuchadnezzar was the first Gentile king to be the ruler of the world. It is no coincidence that the nature of his dream was God's plan for the times of the Gentiles. There are no coincidences in God's planning.

Does God still speak through dreams today? If we have dreams that we think are inspiration, they are more likely to be indigestion. If we think someone can interpret our dreams, we will be spending our money and our time on guesses, speculation, and mostly baloney. We have God's full revelation, and there is a big period at the end of it. He is not speaking through dreams in our time.

The king was determined to have his terrible dream interpreted. His brain trust was made of four different groups: the magicians, who were also scholars; the astrologers, or stargazers; the sorcerers, who were the mediums of their day; and the Chaldeans, who were the wise men of Babylon. With this kind of brain trust in front of him, he wanted them to tell him the meaning of his dream.

An interesting thing happens in the Bible beginning with the fourth verse of the second chapter and concluding at the end of the seventh chapter. Reading through this passage, we find the original language switches from Hebrew to Aramaic. One of the reasons why is that this prophecy deals with the Gentiles; it is written in the language of the Babylonian court. What has Daniel been studying for the past three years? Aramaic, of course. He would have no problem, then, switching from one language to another as he wrote the book bearing his name. Yet another nail in the critic's coffin.

The wise men and soothsayers don't think they'll have any trouble with the dream; all they want to know is what the king dreamed. Now the king has a problem, just as most of us do when we awaken. He couldn't remember his dream! He hadn't forgotten how terrible it was, or how he felt when he was dreaming, but he couldn't remember the details. It's like the feeling we get when we dream we are running away from something or someone, but our legs seem to be on a treadmill going nowhere.

Nebuchadnezzar lowered the axe: "This is what I have firmly decided: If you do not tell me what my dream was and interpret it, I will have you cut into pieces and your houses turned into piles of rubble. But if you tell me the dream and explain it, you will receive from me gifts and rewards and great honor. So tell me the dream and interpret it for me" (Dan. 2:5–6).

All the king's men shook in their sandals. What a preposterous request! Perhaps the king would be reasonable, they thought. "There is not a man on earth who can do what the king asks! No king, however great and mighty, has ever asked such a thing of any magician or enchanter or astrologer. What the king asks is too difficult. No one can reveal it to the king except the gods, and they do not live among men" (Dan. 2:10–11).

This really infuriated the king. He paid this crew to do difficult things, but they were admitting there was no one on earth who, of himself, could describe another's dream.

Why do some people read the Bible and not understand it at all? Why do others find something new and wonderful every time they read it? First Corinthians 2:14 says, "But the natural man receiveth not the things of the Spirit of God: for they are foolishness unto him: neither can he know them, because they are spiritually discerned" (KJV). There stood the religious leaders of Babylon, but they were incapable of unlocking a revelation from God. They said, "There is not a man on earth who can do what the king asks!" (Dan. 2:10). This remark is at the core of the meaning of being a real Christian. Here was Daniel on earth, virtually with connections in heaven, who was able to bring heaven to bear on the things of earth. Those other fellows were out of their league. They were the best that the world had to offer, but they couldn't do the job that had to be done.

The king completely lost it. He was "so angry and furious that he ordered the execution of all the wise men of Babylon. So the decree was issued to put the wise men to death, and men were sent to look for Daniel and his friends to put them to death" (Dan. 2:12–13).

Daniel wasn't even around when the king called in his cabinet of incompetents. But the death penalty was nevertheless upon him. In reality there was more than a violent temper that accounted for this decree. Here was a man who was working under the devices of Satan, and the whole purpose of Satan was to rid the world of Daniel. A man who determines not to compromise his life usually gets Satan's attention.

An old student of the Bible, Graham Scroggie, wrote a powerful analysis of this particular situation, which gives us a better understanding of the battle going on between creationists and evolutionists today:

> Oh, the sin and the folly of pretension. The emphasis is not to be put on Nebuchadnezzar's wrath and cruelty, but on that which occasioned it. These sons of the colleges were trained and paid to interpret mysteries, and it is reasonable to assume that the means whereby they could know the interpretation of a dream might also be employed to discover the dream itself. The fact is, they were frauds. The four Hebrews studied astrology to understand it, not to believe it, just as today the theological student may study evolution to understand it, but not to believe it. Daniel 2:10 shows in one single sentence that all of the astrology and necromancy and oracles and dreams and mantic revelations of the whole pagan world for six thousand years are nothing

but imbecilities and lies, and it proves that all the religions and arts and sciences and philosophies and attainments and powers of men apart from God-inspired prophets and an all-glorious Christ are nothing but emptiness and vanity as regards any true and adequate knowledge of the purpose and will of God.[1]

SECULAR EDUCATION

What happens when Christian parents send their children into a secular environment for their education? The young people are bombarded with information and opinions in all of their subjects, some of which are contrary to God's Word. Even students who are solid in their beliefs may succumb to the pressure of the "wise men" in their classes. When it comes to dealing with the important priorities of life that have to do with the revelation of the Scriptures, we can only find it in a place where godly men stand behind the teaching desk.

Many times I have heard parents say, "I want my child to have the best education in his field, and he can't find that in a Christian school." I do not believe that is true. Many private Christian schools and colleges are academically rigorous, and I strongly urge parents and students to investigate the benefits they provide. Brilliant scholars, who represent the secular viewpoint of their day, haven't graduated from kindergarten when it comes to dealing with the important matters of the kingdom of God.

MAKING FRIENDS WITH THE EXECUTIONER

When the king's cutthroat, Arioch, stormed into Daniel's house, ready to drag him to the gallows as the king commanded, he was greeted graciously by his victim. Daniel knew why he was there;

bad news travels fast. Instead of cowering in the corner like a trapped animal or brandishing a sword in defense, Daniel invited Arioch to sit down and talk things over. "'Why did the king issue such a harsh decree?' Arioch then explained the matter to Daniel" (Dan. 2:15). Isn't it interesting that we have learned Daniel has won his way into the heart of Ashpenaz, and now he has disarmed Arioch. What a guy!

How I would like to be so in control of uncomfortable situations that I could handle each crisis with the poise and composure of Daniel, who calmly went to the king and asked him for a stay of execution that he might interpret the dream. The king's own men had requested more time, but were refused. He had brushed them aside and said, "I am certain that you are trying to gain time" (Dan. 2:8). But Daniel just walked in and said, "Look, I need a little time to decipher this dream," and the king said, "Sure, Daniel, whatever you need."

Daniel needed time not to look up answers in a dream manual, consult the stars, or the nearest psychoanalyst, but to do what all of us should do in tense situations, and that is to pray.

Ruth Bell Graham wrote:

> We are told
> to wait on You.
> But, Lord,
> there is no time.
> My heart implores
> upon its knees,
> "Hurry!
> ... please."[2]

Daniel called on his prayer partners—Hananiah, Mishael, and Azariah—to join him in asking God for answers. "He urged them to plead for mercy from the God of heaven concerning this mystery, so that he and his friends might not be executed with the rest of the wise men of Babylon. During the night the mystery was revealed to Daniel in a vision" (Dan. 2:18–19).

God had given Daniel an unbelievable power to understand dreams and visions, but that gift didn't keep him from praying when the crisis came. He prayed for mercies from heaven, but the best the astrologers could do was get to the stars. Daniel knew the God who made the stars. He went right to the top to get his answer. It is not only useless but also dangerous for Christians to dabble in astrology or to believe daily horoscopes.

During the night God revealed the king's dream to Daniel. I think if I had been Daniel, I probably would have hopped on my camel or chariot and raced to the palace to tell the king immediately. Instead, Daniel had a praise session. He got on his knees and said, "I thank and praise you, O God of my fathers: You have given me wisdom and power, you have made known to me what we asked of you, you have made known to us the dream of the king" (Dan. 2:23). One of the biggest lies we speak as Christians is this one: "And we will be careful to give You thanks. In Jesus' name, Amen." Are we careful? I have tried to discipline myself not to say that any more, because I am finding out that I'm not that careful.

THE SECRET IS OUT

Arioch, the king's henchman, took Daniel over to the palace and announced rather smugly, "I have found a man among the exiles from Judah who can tell the king what his dream means" (Dan. 2:25). No, you didn't, Arioch. He found you! But Arioch was taking credit for something he didn't do, so he couldn't wait to tell the king he had found the answer.

As Daniel began his court appearance, we find that he is not above a little dig at the king's advisers.

> The king asked Daniel . . . "Are you able to tell me what I saw in my dream and interpret it?"
>
> Daniel replied, "No wise man, enchanter, magician or diviner can explain to the king the mystery he has asked about, but there is a God in heaven who reveals mysteries. He has shown King Nebuchadnezzar what will happen in days to come." (Dan. 2:26–28)

Perhaps that sounds a bit cocky, but when you are armed with the power of the Holy Spirit and you walk into the presence of pagans knowing that you are in the will of God, you can be supremely confident. That was Daniel's way. He knew where his power was and He gave God the glory. If he had taken the honor that belonged to God, the story would be over at this point.

As we see the actions of a boy growing into a man, a composite picture of Daniel begins to emerge. He is composed before crisis, courageous before the captain who is to take his life, confident before God in prayer, careful before his success to give praise to the Lord, and when God answers his prayer he is contrite in his spirit.

I think God is just waiting to find some other folks who will fall into that pattern so He can bless them as He blessed Daniel.

God communicated to a pagan king not only the future events in his life, but also in the life of the world. Understanding the prophetic truths in the Bible hinges on the second chapter of Daniel. Doesn't God surprise us with who and what he uses for His purposes? He used a donkey to rebuke the money-loving prophet, Balaam. He commissioned a raven to carry fresh meat to the prophet Elijah. He ordered a rooster to rebuke Peter for backsliding. He can even use you and me!

WHY NOW, GOD?

Why did God choose a time like this, with His people in captivity, to reveal so great a prophecy? If you had been a Jew during that time, you would be wondering, *Is God finished with us? Are we to be put on the shelf forever?* Through a dream and an interpreter, God wanted to say to the Jews, *This isn't the end. There's a future time when I am going to be involved with you again, but I want to tell you what is going to happen in the meantime.*

King Nebuchadnezzar thought he was on the way to being a world conqueror, but God wanted to say, "You may look like you're on top now, but you're just taking one step in the direction of ruin."

DREAM ON

We are not meant to be kept in the dark about Daniel's prophecies. When Jesus was telling His disciples about the signs that would point the way to His Second Coming, He said, "So when you see standing in the holy place 'the abomination that causes desolation,' spoken of through the prophet Daniel—let the reader understand" (Matt. 24:15).

When I read the daily news, I puzzle many times about the actions of man. Why are some acquitted of a heinous crime and others sentenced to years in prison for minor infractions of the law? How can some "musicians" pack auditoriums with their ear-splitting sounds, while true artists play for afternoon concerts that schoolchildren attend on a field day? I don't understand politicians who promise tax cuts and raise taxes, people who have children and abuse them, honor-roll students who drink themselves into a stupor. I don't even try to understand women who shop with no intention to buy, or teenagers who can talk for an hour on the phone without taking a breath.

But God said we could understand prophecy.

What was the king's dream all about? Does it matter to us what a proud, arrogant, evil man dreamed more than twenty-five centuries ago? Jesus told His disciples to pay attention to Daniel. Can we do any less?

King Nebuchadnezzar was probably sitting in his throne room with his head between his hands, dark circles under his eyes, and a troubled expression on his face. In comes this young Jewish captive who claimed to know more than all of his wise men. Well, let him prove himself.

> As you were lying there, O king, your mind turned to things to come, and the revealer of mysteries showed you what is going to happen. As for me, this mystery has been revealed to me, not because I have greater wisdom than other living men, but so that you, O king, may know the interpretation and that you may understand what went through your mind.
>
> You looked, O king, and there before you stood a large statue—an enormous, dazzling statue, awesome in appearance. The head of the statue was made of pure gold, its chest and arms of silver, its belly and thighs of bronze, its legs of iron, its feet partly of iron and partly of baked clay. While you were watching, a rock was cut out, but not by human hands. It struck the statue on its feet of iron and clay and smashed them. Then the iron, the clay, the bronze, the silver and the gold were broken to pieces at the same time and became like chaff on a threshing floor in the summer. The wind swept them away without leaving a trace. But the rock that struck the statue became a huge mountain and filled the whole earth. (Dan. 2:29–35)

Nebuchadnezzar probably stared at Daniel and said, "That's it, I remember now. The statue. That immense statue!"

The image of a man, no matter how gross, was used by God to teach Nebuchadnezzar, Daniel, and us what happens during the days of man when man is in control. This is the history of human civilization, not written by Will Durant or Edward Gibbon, but by God Himself.

Israel, God's own people, except for a remnant, had literally pushed Him aside. They had said, "We don't want you to rule over us." So God allowed the pagan Gentile rulers and kingdoms to move into center stage. The focus of influence moved from Jerusalem to Babylon.

Daniel described this statue as a great image, a gigantic colossus. It was awesome. The colossus of Nebuchadnezzar's dream was a picture of man's perspective on human achievement. Man says, "Look at the advancements we've made in science, space travel, medicine, communication, transportation, genetics, and information. We are so much wiser than our fathers or forefathers." Later on we'll see God's viewpoint of man's achievements.

The dream is the witnessing of the transfer of the world's power from the Jews to the Gentile rulers. We are living today in the times of the Gentiles. Israel is, to this time, being trodden down by the Gentiles, but there is a time coming, and it may be soon, when God's focus will again be on Israel.

The statue symbolizes four empires of the world, kingdoms that have the authority to rule the whole world. Daniel interprets the dream about these kingdoms. These worldwide kingdoms are seen as succeeding one another. Nebuchadnezzar probably broke into a smile, his exhaustion forgotten, when Daniel told him of the first kingdom.

> You, O king, are the king of kings. The God of heaven has given
> you dominion and power and might and glory; in your hands he
> has placed mankind and the beasts of the field and the birds of
> the air. Wherever they live, he has made you ruler over them all.
> You are that head of gold. (Dan. 2:37–38)

Babylon, the golden kingdom, was literally saturated with gold.
When Herodotus, the historian, visited Babylon one hundred years
or so after Nebuchadnezzar, he wrote that in all of his life he had
never seen more gold nor imagined there could be so much. It was
pure glitter from the palace to the Ishtar gate.

The king was enthralled. His ego was inflated, and this unusual
man was causing the tension to melt from his body like a long soak
in a perfumed bath. Nebuchadnezzar lived in more luxury than any
king since Solomon.

Daniel told him:

> After you, another kingdom will rise, inferior to yours. Next,
> a third kingdom, one of bronze, will rule over the whole earth.
> Finally, there will be a fourth kingdom, strong as iron—for iron
> breaks and smashes everything—and as iron breaks things to
> pieces, so it will crush and break all the others. Just as you saw
> that the feet and toes were partly of baked clay and partly of iron,
> so this will be a divided kingdom; yet it will have some of the
> strength of iron in it, even as you saw iron mixed with clay. As
> the toes were partly iron and partly clay, so this kingdom will
> be partly strong and partly brittle. And just as you saw the iron
> mixed with baked clay, so the people will be a mixture and will
> not remain united, any more than iron mixes with clay. (Dan.
> 2:39–43)

History gives us the perspective. How remarkably accurate is the Word of God in every prophetic detail. Follow the description of the "enormous dazzling statue." The second kingdom of silver is Medo-Persia. Later, when the handwriting appears on the wall, this kingdom will be revealed. Notice that there are two arms to the silver section of the image, indicating the divided nature of the second empire. The Medes and the Persians. Together they strong-armed Babylon into submission.

The third kingdom that would rule over the whole earth was Greece. Alexander the Great, the greatest general in ancient times, conquered and ruled the known world of his time. He died at Babylon, his vitality exhausted before he was thirty-three years old. During his lifetime, the soldiers under his command were dressed in bronze and brass helmets, breastplates, shields, and swords.

From the bronze belly and thighs of the colossal statue, we then see the iron legs and feet of the next empire. Every schoolchild has heard of the iron legions of Rome, and, of course, Rome was the ruling empire after Greece.

Fifty years before Jesus was born, the Roman Empire came into existence, and it continued in power during the Lord's earthly ministry. In Gibbon's *The Decline and Fall of the Roman Empire*, he wrote, "The empire of the Romans filled the world, and when the empire fell into the hand of a single person, the world became a dreary prison for his enemies. To resist was fatal, and it was impossible to fly."[3]

It was Roman rule that put Jesus on the cross. It was the imperialistic Romans who ruled ruthlessly throughout the world in the early days of the church. The Roman legions were known for their ability to crush all resistance with an iron heel.

But Daniel told the king that the feet of the statue would be clay, mixed with iron. The Bible clearly teaches that in the end times, during the time of the Antichrist, there will be a ten-kingdom confederacy that rules the world. Many have seen in this prophecy of Daniel's a picture of the renewed Roman Empire in the end times. We are living today in the aftermath of the Roman Empire.

There has been no other world empire since the Romans, so where are we now in God's prophetic picture? We are on the verge of that revived Roman Empire, consisting of ten parts or nations. And where is America in all of this? I don't know. Someone has suggested that when prophecy is fulfilled, America will no longer be in existence or may not be strong enough to be reckoned with as a power. Or the United States may be part of a larger, global community with its roots in Roman law and traditions.

THE MIRACLE OF PROPHECY

When Nebuchadnezzar dreamed this dream, Persia was a Babylonian vassal state, the Greeks were a group of warring tribes, and Rome was a village on the Tiber River. There is no human way he could have seen what God was going to do as those Gentile kingdoms unfolded in the future.

Again we might say, *So what?* When Daniel described the meaning of this bizarre statue, the future kingdoms were identified, but why should that concern us? First of all, the prophecy teaches us something we already know, and that is that human government stands on a delicate foundation. Look at the statue. The gold, silver, bronze, and iron are supported by a mixture that is pure mud. Isn't this a picture of the tottering governments of the earth, with all of their boasted scientific inventions? They are totally unstable. All we need to do is read the newspaper or look at the crumbling governments of the past few years. They are built on the unstable foundation of humanistic ideas, which is unpredictable and weak.

The second thing we learn from the statue is that human

government is deteriorating. The application of this dream to our day is frightening. The descending scale of value from gold to clay suggests that the degeneration of the human race throughout the ages is prevalent. Each kingdom is built on the ruins of the one before. This should strike a blow to the evolutionist, who has the image standing on its head, with everything getting better and better. Does anyone really believe the world is getting better?

The metals—from gold to silver to bronze to iron—are deteriorating. The specific gravity of gold is 19.3, silver is 10.5, bronze is 8.5, iron is 7.6, and clay is 1.9. What a striking proof of what happens when everything human gets off the gold standard.

The power of the governments is represented by the statue. Babylon was a monarchy, ruled with an iron hand by Nebuchadnezzar. The Medes and Persians had an oligarchic form of government, which is government ruled by a few men. The Grecian form of government was aristocratic, rule by the nobility. Finally, Rome was an imperialistic government. It was military and ruthless, like Nazi Germany.

In God's mind, democracy is not His kind of government. I am the most patriotic person you could imagine, and I wouldn't want to live anyplace but America, but God's government isn't a democracy. It's a monarchy. That monarchy, which He will set up someday, will be a theocracy, ruled by God alone.

The reason we have democracy is because we don't have righteous-rule monarchy. We need some kind of checks and balances, which is why our government is established as it is.

When the thirteen colonies were still a part of England, Scottish Professor Alexander Tytler wrote about the fall of the Athenian Republic over a thousand years before. He said:

A democracy cannot exist as a permanent form of government. It can only exist until the voters discover that they can vote themselves money from the public treasure. From that moment on the majority always votes for the candidates promising the most money from the public treasury, with the result that a democracy always collapses over loose fiscal policy followed by a dictatorship. The average age of the world's great civilizations has been two hundred years. These nations have progressed through the following sequence: from bondage to spiritual faith, from spiritual faith to great courage, from courage to liberty, from liberty to abundance, from abundance to selfishness, from selfishness to complacency, from complacency to apathy, from apathy to dependency, from dependency back to bondage.[4]

Where are we? We have a deteriorating form of government, no matter what party is elected or who is president.

The third prophetic picture from the statue, after the delicate foundation and the deteriorating form of human government, is the disintegrating family of government. This does not refer to a personal family, but the family of nations. In the stream of humanity there are two conflicting elements: the iron will of authority and the claylike voice of the people. As we near the end of the age, this struggle will get greater and greater, pulling nations apart. People will rise against governments; authority will try to quell the voice of the people. This will increase in the coming days.

Finally, the prophecy of the statue shows the developing force of human government. Look down the image and see how each metal, from gold to silver to bronze to iron, increases in strength. It is an overwhelming thought to realize that as we degenerate in morality, we increase in force.

All of this reminds us that we are living on the threshold of the end of the age. Just when we begin to be depressed, we are told of the rock "cut out of a mountain, but not by human hands—a rock that broke the iron, the bronze, the clay, the silver and the gold to pieces" (Dan. 2:45). This is the Lord Jesus coming in His glory to destroy all world governments and, like a mountain, fill the whole earth.

In 1886, Franklin Belden wrote "Look for the Way-Marks" as a reminder to be ready for Christ's return:

> Look for the way-marks as you journey on,
> Look for the way-marks passing one by one;
> Down through the ages past the kingdoms four,
> Where are we standing?
> Look the way-marks o'er.
> Down in the feet of iron and of clay,
> Weak and divided, soon to pass away;
> What will the next great, glorious drama be?
> Christ and His coming and eternity![5]

"The great God has shown the king what will take place in the future" (Dan. 2:45), and aren't we fortunate that He's told us too!

5

WHEN CHRIST RULES
THE WORLD

Daniel 2 teaches us very clearly that one thing is certain: the kingdoms of this world are passing away, and the kingdom of Christ is the only hope we have of an eternal and successful world rule. When that kingdom comes, it is going to be a different story than what we hear today. The devil seems to be writing history now, but he will be history in the near future.

As the king's dream is being described by Daniel, the climax is reached when the great stone is detached from a mountain and begins to move toward the image with great speed. It strikes the image at the feet and crushes it to powder. The question is, who or what is the stone?

IDENTITY OF THE STONE

We are not left to guess the identification of the stone. Over fourteen times in the Scriptures Jesus is referred to as the stone. Several times He is called the *smitten stone*. In the book of Exodus, when

Moses smote the rock (Ex. 17:5–6), water gushed forth. In the New Testament, Paul interprets this miraculous prophecy: "They all ate the same spiritual food and drank the same spiritual drink; for they drank from the spiritual rock that accompanied them, and that rock was Christ" (1 Cor. 10:3–4). The smitten stone of Exodus becomes a picture of the smitten Christ on the cross. It was there that He was the fountainhead of blessing as His blood gushed forth and He became the Redeemer of the world.

Christ is also the *stumbling stone*. The apostle Paul quoted the prophet Isaiah: "See, I lay in Zion a stone that causes men to stumble and a rock that makes them fall, and the one who trusts in him will never be put to shame" (Rom. 9:33, from Isa. 8:14; 28:16).

Next, He is a *special stone*. In every stone building there is one stone that is crucial. It is the stone upon which the weight of the whole structure rests. It is sometimes called the special stone, or the cornerstone. Jesus is referred to as the cornerstone, or the stone upon which the weight of the house rests. Isaiah wrote: "See, I lay a stone in Zion, a tested stone, a precious cornerstone for a sure foundation; the one who trusts will never be dismayed" (Isa. 28:16). How could Isaiah, who lived more than seven hundred years before Christ, describe the characteristics of Jesus so accurately? Because he was one of God's greatest prophets.

I find that studying prophecy is endlessly fascinating. Over and over again we discover that this one who is the stone is Jesus Christ. Now Daniel says He is also the *smiting stone*. He is going to come and destroy the image which represents the world governments of our day. What a blow to Nebuchadnezzar! In his mind's eye he sees a stone rolling down the mountain like a gold-medal Olympic skier and pulverizing the image. The stone then fills the whole earth, which depicts the coming kingdom of Christ.

A LOOK AT THE COMING KINGDOM

The kingdom of Christ that will come in the end times is a supernatural kingdom. The Scripture says that this stone that becomes the mountain is cut without hands; it is not manmade. We can make bricks. We can build superstructures and skyscrapers. But only God can make a stone. No human hand fashioned the substance of Christ; He was implanted in the womb of Mary by the Holy Spirit and resurrected from the grave by His own power. He is coming one day to establish a supernatural kingdom, something unlike anything we have ever known.

His kingdom will be sudden. All of the other kingdoms of the dream image—Babylon, Medo-Persia, Greece, and Rome—were built on one another and were gradual in the making. Christ's kingdom will come with a sudden and decisive blow. He is not going to sneak up on us. Students of prophecy understand that the Second Coming of Christ will be in two phases: first, the Rapture of the church will remove all believers before the Tribulation, and second, the Second Advent, which takes place predictably at the end of the seven years of Tribulation. According to Revelation, all believers will return with Christ to set up His kingdom on earth.

When Christ comes to set up His kingdom, every eye shall see him. "At that time the sign of the Son of Man will appear in the sky, and all the nations of the earth will mourn. They will see the Son of Man coming on the clouds of the sky, with power and great glory" (Matt. 24:30). This is the Second Advent, not the Rapture, and it will be an event that is not only supernatural and sudden, but also severe.

Especially at Christmas we sing about the baby Jesus, but He is also the righteous judge. One day this old world that has rejected Him, made Him a laughingstock among the nations, and used His name as a swear word will see Him come back riding on a white horse, and He will deal a deathblow to the nations.

The prophet Malachi gave a chilling description of the time when Christ would return to set up His kingdom. "'Surely the day is coming; it will burn like a furnace. All the arrogant and every evildoer will be stubble, and that day that is coming will set them on fire,' says the LORD Almighty" (Mal. 4:1).

When Jesus returns, the Scripture says He is going to rule over all the earth. The mountain that Daniel saw filling the universe is the sovereign rule of King Jesus. Psalm 72:11 says, "All kings will bow down to him and all nations will serve him."

Christ's kingdom will also be successful. There will be no revolutions, no political campaigns or party systems, and no decay. He will be a monarch without a successor, and it will be a kingdom without end. No dictator, uprising, or political *coup d'état* will oust this ruler. His kingdom will endure forever. When Daniel says that, it means for an age, which sometimes means for a specific age, which Revelation tells us will be a thousand years, or a millennium.

WHAT TO BELIEVE ABOUT THE MILLENNIUM

Can history boast of a supernatural, sudden, severe, sovereign, and successful kingdom? It has never been achieved. Many have tried, but all have failed. However, there is a group of theologians who like to tell us that it happened in another way. They call themselves amillennialists, which means that they don't believe there will be a Millennium or that there is ever going to be a kingdom. They say that it is the kingdom of Christ ruling and reigning in our hearts, and that the church of Jesus Christ is the kingdom. The amillennialists say that we are becoming the kingdom of Christ by taking control of the world through conversion, but the Bible says when the

King comes, it's going to be sudden. The only way the amillennialists could explain this prophecy is to say that when Jesus comes, the whole world will become Christian.

A second test for our amillennial friends is to explain how the church, or the Christians, could be the kingdom of Christ if His coming is to be severe. The third test comes in the sovereignty of the kingdom. When Christ rules upon this earth there will be no free will for His subjects. Every knee shall bow and every tongue shall confess. There is certainly no evidence, nineteen hundred years after Christ, that the kingdom has conquered the world.

And explain this: the kingdom of Christ is to be successful. However, today the rate of conversion does not keep up with the birthrate. We aren't gaining ground; we're losing. If this is the kingdom that is supposed to fill the whole earth, we're going backward.

WHERE I STAND

I believe that Jesus Christ is coming back "pre" or before the Millennium, and that He is going to establish the Millennium after He comes back. The Millennium isn't going to make this world fit for the Lord to return; He will be here to establish it Himself. It is important to know what we believe, not just to consider this an issue to be left to theorizing and guessing.

When I see the bumper stickers and T-shirts proclaiming "Peace Now," I smile and think, *We must do our best to keep the peace so we can preach the gospel, but we can't stop all war until Jesus comes back and ends it all.*

Christ will come back when He is ready, and He will set up His kingdom without our help. That's why we need to be praying this great prayer with Isaiah: "Oh, that you would rend the heavens and come down" (Isa. 64:1). And on the Isle of Patmos we can say with

John, "Amen. Come, Lord Jesus" (Rev. 22:20). That's the only hope for lasting peace.

Charles Wesley took Isaiah's prayer and John's statement and wrote a great hymn that is seldom sung in our churches today.

Lo, He comes with clouds descending,
Once for favored sinners slain;
Thousand thousand saints attending
Swell the triumph of His train.
Alleluia! Alleluia!
God appears on earth to reign.

Now the Savior, long expected,
See in solemn pomp appear.
All His saints by man rejected,
Now shall meet Him in the air.
Alleluia! Alleluia!
See the day of God appear.

Yes, amen! Let all adore Thee,
High on Thine eternal throne.
Savior, take the pow'r and glory;
Claim the kingdom for Thine own.
O come quickly, O come quickly!
Everlasting God, come down.[1]

My heart sings the same song when I view the world today. Does that mean I don't get involved in trying to make this place better? No, of course not. But it does mean I'm realistic about any hope that we have of ultimate success. If we can do anything with our lives, we should be preparing people for the coming of the King the first time to take His saints out of this world. When He comes the second time to rule and reign, there are going to be a lot of folks who aren't a part of the kingdom now who will be part of the eternal kingdom because we have had some influence in their lives.

WHEN IS CHRIST GOING TO RETURN?

I am not a date setter. However, the next event on the horizon is the Rapture, then the Tribulation period for seven years, followed by the return of Christ at the end of the Tribulation. We may be as close as seven years away from the kingdom of Christ. There are only two things I know of that have to happen: the shout and the trumpet. "For the Lord himself will come down from heaven, with a loud command, with the voice of the archangel and with the trumpet call of God, and the dead in Christ will rise first. After that, we who are still alive and are left will be caught up together with them in the clouds to meet the Lord in the air. And so we will be with the Lord forever" (1 Thess. 4:16–17).

After that the Tribulation will break out, and at the end of seven years the Lord will return with His saints to wipe out the chaos and set up His kingdom.

I want to make it clear, however, that there's no second chance after the Rapture for those who have heard the Word of God and rejected Christ (see 2 Thess. 2:9–10). There is only one chance, and it is here and now. God has given us two options: we can bow down to Him now in saving faith, or someday we will bow down to Him as the sovereign King. We can bow down to Him now and ask Him to be the Lord of our lives, or we can reject Him and someday be an unwilling subject of the King, to be judged by Him and sent to an unseemly eternal destination.

As a minister I frequently have people say to me something like,

"I don't want to be told I'll go to hell if I don't accept Christ." Well, I don't like telling people they'll go to hell either. But that's the way it is. No amount of kind deeds, philanthropies, or decent conduct will give us a ticket to heaven.

NEBUCHADNEZZAR ON HIS KNEES

When Daniel finished the interpretation of Nebuchadnezzar's dream, the king came off his throne and onto the floor. He said he believed Daniel's God was the God of gods. Whether that profession was real or not, we will never know until we get to heaven. But at that moment he at least mouthed the words.

Instead of a death sentence, Daniel received a court position. From that time on, he was a government leader who was never turned out of office. When Daniel was placed in charge of the wise men, he made a few appointments himself. He probably thought, *All of these mystics and astrologers and sorcerers are not going to be much help to me. I'll bring in my own crew.* So Shadrach, Meshach, and Abednego were appointed administrators over the province of Babylon, and Daniel remained in the royal court.

Daniel's three friends will be remembered until history ends. But the true story of their experience is more remarkable than any fictionalized account in books and song.

6

FIERY FAITH

I n the late 1960s there was a man—a leader in terrorist activities and an advocate of the violent overthrow of the American government—who escaped the police to become an exile in France. It was there that he claimed to see Jesus in the clouds and became a born-again believer. He returned to America, prepared to face criminal charges and proclaim his conversion to the media and packed churches. Sometime later it was reported that he had joined the cult of Sun Myung Moon.

When someone who is well-known makes a radical confession of faith, one of the first things that often happens is an appearance on television or the church circuit. But many times, before we know it, they have embarrassed us by something they have said or done. We need to use the test of time before we elevate any person as a role model—including celebrities.

Nebuchadnezzar was a vocal witness of his faith in the Lord, but when we hear about him in the third chapter of Daniel, we're not too impressed. According to the Septuagint's (the oldest Greek version of the Old Testament) account of this passage, there were somewhere between sixteen and twenty years between the end of chapter two and the beginning of chapter three. So Nebuchadnezzar had plenty of time to rethink his impulsive commitment to the Lord and revive his own egomania.

IMAGE IN THE DESERT

The king ordered his head masons, designers, and gold embossers to erect a statue in his image. He had become so impressed with the dream he had that he must have reasoned, *If I am the head of gold, why not be the whole body?* This statue was not like the ones we see in the middle of a public park; it was a colossal, grotesque, shining monstrosity. The Scripture says it was sixty cubits high and six cubits wide. That's ninety feet tall! It was also unbalanced (just as the king's mind). The ratio of the image was ten-to-one, which means it was a skinny, skinny man. The average body ratio of a person today is five-to-one. All that gold, shimmering in the sun, could have been seen for miles away.

A guest list, consisting of the cream of Babylonian society, was prepared. "He then summoned the satraps, prefects, governors, advisers, treasurers, judges, magistrates and all the other provincial officials to come to the dedication of the image he had set up" (Dan. 3:2). Everyone accepted. It was an example of peer pressure at the highest level. The only one of the officials who was absent was Daniel, and he had probably been sent elsewhere on a mission by the king. That seemingly insignificant detail has its purpose in God's ultimate plan.

It was no coincidence that the designers of this bizarre statue made it sixty cubits high and six cubits wide. In Revelation 13:18, the number of the beast of the Antichrist was the number of man, 666. The Bible gives the number six to mankind; seven is the number for perfection. We fall short; we never come up to the standard.

The image is a good picture of mankind; it was made of wood overlaid with gold. That's the way our projects are: outwardly imperishable, but inwardly inferior. Man is always setting up his gigantic projects, but when you get down to the core of them, there's not much there.

The basic reason King Nebuchadnezzar had this image set up in the desert is that he was doing his best to unite his kingdom religiously. He ruled over a vast empire, and he decided the way to unify his empire was to bring it together through religion and have everyone bow down before this image. In the end times this is what the Antichrist is going to do.

The second thing the king did was deify himself. When we study history we discover that the great egomaniacs who have wanted to conquer the world have been men who have tried to use religion for their own purposes. In the late 1930s, it was written:

One cannot be a good German and at the same time deny God. But an avowal of faith in the eternal Germany is an avowal of faith in the eternal God. Whoever serves Adolf Hitler the Führer serves Germany, and whoever serves Germany serves God.[1]

Later on, in 1942, this was written:

There is a lot of talk in Germany about Hitler's Messianic characteristics. The thesis that Hitler is a miraculous being sent by a Supreme Power, and that he is capable of mystic communion with the German masses is gaining greater currency. Consequently, the attack on Christian religion becomes more severe. In Germany, no attempt is made to stamp out the faith in the supernatural. The policy is more blasphemous. It is to replace Christ. Religion is now counterfeited rather than dismissed. This extraordinary tendency is perhaps without parallel during the last two thousand years. The Nazis are trying to create an anti-type of Christianity. They have made their leader their God.[2]

We know that is historically true. Nebuchadnezzar was trying to unify the people around his image.

When this mass of humanity was gathered on the Plain of Dura, shading their eyes from the reflection of the beating desert sun on the golden image, the king gave orders to his professional preacher, a herald with a loud voice. As all false gods have their pulpiteers, the king had this man who told the crowd what he was paid to say. He announced that when the orchestra played, everybody had to hit the ground. Worship or burn were the only options.

The orchestra was a weird bunch; they never would have made it to a philharmonic. Everything from a harp to bagpipes sounded the dissonant notes for worship. I believe this is one of the early indications in the Word of God of the prostitution of music. Almost every major cult and -ism, every false religion, has found some way to use music for its perverted purposes. It's a type of mind control. I believe with all my heart that music belongs to God. It belongs to the angels. It belongs to God's people. The world will take what belongs to God and prostitute it for its own purposes.

The band played and the crowd (someone has estimated there were as many as three hundred thousand people from all of the vast empire) hit the dust. All of them, that is, but three. Can you image how they stuck out when thousands and thousands of people were on the ground and they alone were standing?

It reminds me of an experience my wife, Donna, and I had as newlyweds. We had a lot of good friends in college, and we used to do some interesting things to them when they were about to get married. One time, for instance, we managed to get the key to our friends' apartment while they were on their honeymoon, and we went in and took all the labels off the cans. For six months, every meal was an adventure. "Will it be dog food or peaches tonight?"

When we announced our wedding, we knew there would be some retribution. One thing I thought would be a target was our car. I had a 1961 red Chevy Impala convertible with a white roof. It was the pride and joy of our lives in those early days, and I knew somebody was going to try to get it. However, I thought I could outmaneuver them. I went to a shopping center near where we were to be married and parked it right in the middle of the parking lot. There must have been two thousand cars at that location. They would never find it, I thought.

That night after the wedding I went to retrieve our car, and there was my red-and-white Impala convertible all alone in the middle of the lot. The shopping center closed at 5 P.M.

I think the three Hebrew men stuck out in the crowd more than my lonely car.

CONSPIRACY OF THE WISE MEN

Now the plot begins to thicken. The astrologers came out and bowed before Nebuchadnezzar, reminding him that he had ordered everyone to bow down. Perhaps the king had bad eyesight. How could he help but notice that there were three traitors who paid no attention to the order?

Solomon said, "Jealousy . . . burns like blazing fire, like a mighty flame" (Song of Sol. 8:6), and the Chaldean crowd wanted to smell the seared flesh of Shadrach, Meshach, and Abednego.

Nebuchadnezzar was furious. He commanded the three Hebrews to be brought before him and repeated his order. This time he didn't assign his paid preacher to announce the worship moment;

he gave it himself. He said, "Now, when you hear the sound of the horn, flute, zither, lyre, harp, pipes and all kinds of music, if you are ready to fall down and worship the image I made, very good. But if you do not worship it, you will be thrown immediately into a blazing furnace. Then what god will be able to rescue you from my hand?" (Dan. 3:15).

The orchestra members had their instruments poised and waited for the baton to come down on the first beat. Thousands of eyes must have been boring into the backs of the three Hebrews as they stood before the king. In the minds of the doomed ones was the realization that there was really no option for them. They knew the Old Testament law that speaks clearly about idolatry. "You shall not make for yourself an idol in the form of anything in heaven above or on the earth beneath or in the waters below. You shall not bow down to them or worship them" (Exod. 20:4–5). The choice was between the king's command and God's Word.

Idolatry is not only the worship of false gods, but also the worship of the true God by images. John Calvin, the great theologian, said, "A true image of God is not to be found in all of the world; and hence that His glory is defiled, and His truth corrupted by the lie, whenever He is set before our eyes in a visible form. . . . Therefore, to devise any image of God, is in itself impious; because by this corruption His majesty is adulterated, and He is figured to be other than He is."[3]

A lot of idolatry goes on in our day—not just in the church but also in the marketplace. God is not interested in being worshiped through something; He wants to be worshiped in spirit and in truth. Wearing a cross or a crucifix will not make a person a Christian, nor is it always honoring to the Lord.

The king was willing to give them another chance if they would reconsider their disobedient attitude, but he made it clear that he would carry out the punishment if they refused. We can hear the sarcasm in his voice when he asks them, "What god will be able to rescue you?" How soon he has forgotten that it was that God who honored him with a wonderful dream that Daniel had been able to interpret. It was that God who made known the whole history of the world to him. That God created Nebuchadnezzar, protected him, clothed and fed him, and honored him with the rulership of the first world empire. He had forgotten that God, but in a few years he was going to experience the power of that God to bring him to his knees.

The history of the church has been written in blood. There will always be warfare between the powers of darkness and the powers of light, and there will always be pagan rulers who will cry out in sarcasm, *Who is that god?*

One of the greatest statements of faith in the Bible is the response of these three men. It thrills me to read it:

Shadrach, Meshach and Abednego replied to the king, "O Nebuchadnezzar, we do not need to defend ourselves before you in this matter. If we are thrown into the blazing furnace, the God we serve is able to save us from it, and he will rescue us from your hand, O king. But even if he does not, we want you to know, O king, that we will not serve your gods or worship the image of gold you have set up." (Dan. 3:16–18)

They had a word from God and that's all they needed. The path of duty was plain; they didn't have to think about it or have a committee meeting. What an example!

This is what this world is crying for: men and women, boys and girls, who have conviction of heart and who do not change their convictions on the basis of their circumstances. These three men knew what God wanted them to do, and they weren't afraid of the consequences.

Athanasius was one of the early church fathers. We are indebted to him for the purity of the doctrine of the deity of Jesus Christ. The story is told that someone came to him and said, "Athanasius, don't you know that the emperor is against you, the bishops are against you, the church is against you, and the whole world is against you?" Athanasius answered, "Then I am against the whole world." A phrase was coined that became rather famous in the early church: *Athanasius against the whole world.*

Studdert Kennedy was a chaplain during World War I. He was often thrust into the frontlines of battle, ministering in places of danger to his life. One day as he was going through France, he wrote a letter to his son, who was about ten years old. This is what he wrote to his little boy:

> The first prayer I want my son to learn to say for me is not, "God, keep Daddy safe," but, "God make Daddy brave. And if he has hard things to do, make him strong to do them."
>
> Son, life and death don't matter. But right and wrong do. Daddy dead is Daddy still, but Daddy dishonored before God is something too awful for words. I suppose you would like to put in a bit about safety, too, and Mother would like that, I'm sure. Well, put it in afterwards, for it really doesn't matter nearly as much as doing what is right.[4]

We don't know if Shadrach, Meshach, and Abednego had ever played fast and loose with what was right, but we do know that they had some pretty solid training in God's law.

When those three responded to the king, he blew up. His pride was wounded, his will had been crossed, and he was so mad he exploded. King Nebuchadnezzar is an interesting study. He was a man of superlatives: the biggest image, the most expensive gold, the most lavish party. He could put on a real show. When he pronounced judgment, it had to be the worst he could think of, and that was being burned alive in the furnace. But if that weren't enough, he said, "Throw in the coal! Make it seven times hotter! Turn on the heat!" Then he picked the strongest soldiers in his army to tie up the Hebrews so they couldn't move. The king was so furious that he was out of control.

It's curious that this furnace would be out in the middle of the desert, but it makes us wonder if the king hadn't planned ahead for what he would do if he was disobeyed. The furnace was a big potbellied structure with a large opening in the top. The victims were to be thrown in from above. When the soldiers pushed the Hebrews to the top of the furnace, the fire was so hot that the captors were turned to ashes before Shadrach, Meshach, and Abednego fell in. If that weren't enough to shock the partygoers, the next sight must have made their eyes pop.

The king's roller-coaster emotions were enough to give a man a heart attack.

Then King Nebuchadnezzar leaped to his feet in amazement and asked his advisers, "Weren't there three men that we tied up and threw into the fire?"

They replied, "Certainly, O king."

He said, "Look! I see four men walking around in the fire, unbound and unharmed, and the fourth looks like a son of the gods." (Dan. 3:24–25)

It must have been with great caution, heart beating fast, and perspiration dripping from his face that the king approached the opening of the furnace and shouted, "Shadrach, Meshach and Abednego, servants of the Most High God, come out!"

The three walked out of the furnace, probably stepping over the charred remains of the guards, and stood before their accusers, calm and well-groomed. Their clothes and hair were untouched, and they didn't even smell of smoke.

King Nebuchadnezzar, true to his impulsive and erratic nature, said, "Praise be to the God of Shadrach, Meshach and Abednego, who has sent his angel and rescued his servants! They trusted in him and defied the king's command and were willing to give up their lives rather than serve or worship any god except their own God" (Dan. 3:28).

With customary harshness, the king ordered that anyone who said anything against the God of the Hebrews was to be cut into pieces and their houses burned. Just as he had done with Daniel, he sent the uncompromising Hebrew trio from the firing line to the frontline.

WHY WEREN'T THEY HURT?

Why does God save some and not others? Why does an innocent baby die and a murderer go free? We constantly wrestle with those questions. I do not have the answers; however, I believe God teaches through His book and through the stories of His children. When our Hebrew friends refused to bow to the statue, they expressed their absolute commitment to God. They didn't need to discuss it, have a conference call, or negotiate.

They also had absolute confidence in God. "We know God can deliver us from the fiery furnace." They also recognized that God's will might be different from their desire, but they didn't make their own obedience contingent upon God doing what would be pleasing to them. Here is where we fall far short of this standard. We pray, "Lord, just get me out of this mess, and I'll do whatever you wish."

We make tearful promises to try to negotiate a contract with the Lord. But here were men who didn't try to rewrite the script. They just said, "Lord, we don't know how You are going to do it. We don't even know for sure what You're going to do, but we believe in You."

Stories of courage inspire us, but seldom do we see such absolute courage for God as was shown by the Hebrews. Whenever we have a hard assignment from God, there seems to be a list of reasons why we shouldn't do it. The three Hebrews didn't even have Daniel for support. He was out of town, probably on the king's business in another province. They were in a situation where they had great opportunity to move up into the hierarchy of the Babylonian kingdom. If they defied the king, obviously they wouldn't get promoted. They might have rationalized (and many of us are so good at that) by saying, "Lord, you need us in places of responsibility. Bowing down isn't such a big deal, is it?" If that had been their rationale, we never would have heard of them. They would have been part of the vast army of unknowns. History does not usually elevate acts of cowardice.

It has been said that when the executioner went behind Jerome of Prague, one of Christendom's early martyrs, to set fire to the pile where he was chained, Jerome said, "Come here and kindle the fire before my eyes, for if I had dreaded such a sight I would never have come to such a place when I had the free opportunity to escape." The fire was kindled in front of him, and he began to sing a hymn that was soon finished by the flames that consumed him. Absolute courage.

Martin Luther, when he was on his way to be excommunicated, appeared before King Charles V and an assemblage of princes and said:

My cause shall be commended to the Lord, for He lives and reigns who preserved the three children in the furnace of the Babylonian king. If He is unwilling to preserve me, my life is a small thing compared with Christ. Expect anything of me except flight or recantation. I will not flee, much less recant, so may the Lord Jesus strengthen me.[5]

The Hebrews were absolutely conscious of the presence of God. When they were walking around in the fiery furnace, they were talking with the Lord. They knew the Lord before, and He was present with them. Isaiah prophesied (150 years earlier), "When you walk through the fire, you will not be burned; the flames will not set you ablaze" (Isa. 43:2). Incidentally, this passage does not validate a fire-walking experience today. Please don't try it.

I have found in my own life, and from what many people have told me, that when we are in the hottest furnace of our trials we are more conscious of the Lord's presence than at any other time in our lives. In the process of our personal fires, God takes care of our enemies too. The guards who threw them into the furnace went up in flames themselves.

The fire served to burn the cords with which they were bound and set them free. Many times when the fire is so hot for us that we think we are going to be consumed, we come out of it liberated from the things we worried about.

When King Nebuchadnezzar saw the fourth form in the fire, he actually saw Christ hundreds of years before His virgin birth. What an astounding thought! Whenever His children are in the fire, He is there too. He was with Moses who saw Him in the burning bush, with the disciples in the midst of the storm at sea, and with Stephen as he was being stoned by an angry mob.

This story is a wonderful illustration of the willingness of God to involve Himself in the affairs of His people. It seems to me that He comes into our trials and troubles more than any other circumstance of life. He stands with the person who has lost a loved one, and if they are Christians they will say, "I have never felt the presence of the Lord like I have in these past days."

God uses our problem times to wake us up so that He might move into our lives. It seems like there are more problem areas today than there have been for the past decade. Maybe God has heated up the furnace in our lives just enough to get our attention. He doesn't promise to save us from the fire, but to be with us through the fire.

Through it all, God was exalted. First, the big, loudmouth king said, "Look, I'm going to throw you into this fiery furnace and see if your God can deliver you." But when he looked into the fire and saw God's presence, protection, and power, he praised the very God he had previously mocked.

People see God in us when we are in the fire. It's easy to be a Christian when everything is going great, but when the fire is hot, we are being watched.

I remember one time asking a couple how they came to know Christ, and they said:

> We lived next door to a certain couple in our church, and it was at a time when all of the factories in our area were shutting down. People were being laid off every day and things were real tough. This particular Christian couple had been without work for over six months. All of their benefits had run out and they were just eking out an existence. We watched them as God literally took away everything they had. We saw them praising the Lord, having smiles on their faces and never complaining. One night after supper we were talking about them, and we said, "Whatever they had, that's what we needed." We went over to their house and they led us to Christ.

They saw God in the fire.

The last thing that happened to Shadrach, Meshach, and Abednego is that their influence was enlarged. The king promoted them. When God tests us and we prove faithful, it is always for the purpose of enlarging our influence for Him.

The Bible says: "Be faithful, even to the point of death, and I will give you the crown of life" (Rev. 2:10).

"Now if we are children, then we are heirs—heirs of God and co-heirs with Christ, if indeed we share in his sufferings in order that we may also share in his glory" (Rom. 8:17).

John Chrysostom was one of the greatest of the Greek church fathers. He lived in AD 347–407. As a very young Christian he was brought before the emperor, who said that if he would not give up Christ, he would be banished from the country.

Chrysostom said, "You cannot, for the whole world is my Father's land. You can't banish me."

The emperor said, "Then I will take away all your property."

"You cannot. My treasures are in heaven," was the reply.

"Then I'll take you to a place where there is not a friend to speak to."

Chrysostom replied, "You cannot. I have a friend who is closer than a brother. I shall have Jesus Christ, forever."

The emperor finally threatened, "Then I'll take away your life!"

The answer was, "You cannot. My life is hid with God in Christ."

And the emperor said, "What do you do with a man like that?"

Obviously, I do not know the rest of that historical conversation, but this ought to be the way it is for all of us who are Christians. When we are tested in the fiery furnace, the world should say, "What do you do with a person like that?"

7

THE GOSPEL ACCORDING
TO NEBUCHADNEZZAR

Napoleon is portrayed by the artists he commissioned to memorialize him as a strutting little man, standing defiantly with his right hand pushed between his vest buttons or as a hero astride a fiery steed, pointing the way for his troops to cross the Alps. His bicorn hat made him instantly recognizable and imitated at costume parties through the years. He was proud, a man driven by ambition to conquer Europe.

The story is told that on the morning of the battle of Waterloo, Napoleon was describing to his commanding officer his strategy for that day's campaign. He said, "We'll put the infantry here, the cavalry over there, and the artillery in that spot. At the end of the day, England will be at the feet of France, and Wellington will be the prisoner of Napoleon."

The commanding officer responded, "But we must not forget that man proposes and God disposes."

With typical arrogance, the little dictator pulled his body to its full five-feet-two and replied, "I want you to understand, sir, that Napoleon proposes and Napoleon disposes."

Victor Hugo, the novelist, reportedly wrote, "From that moment, Waterloo was lost, for God sent rain and hail so that the troops of Napoleon could not maneuver as he had planned, and on the night of battle it was Napoleon who was prisoner of Wellington, and France was at the feet of England."

If you asked me what the most fundamental sin is, I would answer without hesitation: the sin of pride. Pride is basic to all other sins. It is simply exaggerated and dishonest self-evaluation. It was the sin that began sin, when Satan said, "I will be like the Most High God."

Pride is number one on God's hate list. "These six things doth the LORD hate: yea, seven are an abomination unto him: A proud look" (Prov. 6:16–17 KJV).

Proverbs hits the issue of pride hard:

- "The LORD detests all the proud of heart" (16:5).
- "I hate pride and arrogance, evil behavior and perverse speech" (8:13).
- "Pride goes before destruction, a haughty spirit before a fall" (16:18).
- "When pride comes, then comes disgrace" (11:2).

If we summarize all the Old Testament proverbs, we could easily do it with one key verse from the New Testament: "God opposes the proud but gives grace to the humble" (James 4:6).

THE PERSONAL LETTER OF A KING

The fourth chapter of Daniel contains a unique Babylonian state document, written by Nebuchadnezzar himself. It is his personal testimony of how God took him from where he was to where God wanted him to be, and Nebuchadnezzar tells in his own language exactly how God dealt with him.

Interesting individual, Nebuchadnezzar. From Daniel 2 and 3 we might get the idea that he was warm to spiritual matters. He was given a couple of warnings, however, that just a tip of his hat to God did not mean he was ready to bow down and worship. When God showed him through Daniel that he was the head of gold in the image, he was warned that the image that represented the kingdoms of this world was only going to exist for a short time. But that red light wasn't enough to stop him.

When he saw God in the fire, Nebuchadnezzar made a shallow commitment, but he never really repented. In the fourth chapter of Daniel, the proud king tells us what is going to happen to him. He has run all of the stop lights, and now he is caught and arrested.

> King Nebuchadnezzar,
>> To the peoples, nations and men of every language, who live
> in all the world:
>> May you prosper greatly!
>> It is my pleasure to tell you about the miraculous signs and
> wonders that the Most High God has performed for me.
>
>> How great are his signs,
>> how mighty his wonders!
>> His kingdom is an eternal kingdom;
>> his dominion endures from generation to generation.
>>> (Dan. 4:1–3)

The introduction is written by none other than the king himself. Here is a monarch at the peak of his popularity, giving a universal declaration. If he had lived in our day, his testimony would have gone out on social media and the 24/7 cable news networks.

The testimony was very personal. He was not talking about what God did in somebody else's life, but what God had done toward him. He didn't stand at a podium and mumble, he shared his testimony with enthusiasm. He wanted the whole world to know what God had done for him.

ANOTHER NIGHTMARE

Nebuchadnezzar recounts another dream and says that he was in his palace, feeling contented with life, having plenty of money in the Babylonian Trust and Savings, and facing no war to threaten this condition. He was proud of his accomplishments, including the wondrous Hanging Gardens of Babylon, which he had built as a love gift for his beautiful wife. How could any man wish for more? But he began to dream again, and the old fear of the strange night images troubled him like some ghostly apparition in a haunted castle. So what did he do? *Oh, Nebuchadnezzar, will you never learn?* He called all of the magicians, enchanters, astrologers, and diviners who couldn't interpret his dream before, and they were no better this time. You would have thought the king wouldn't waste any more time on these charlatans.

It has been said that no matter how often the wisdom of the world fails, we run right back to the same people who have never had the answers. We go to these secular-humanist counselors, who don't help, and then finally find a Christian counselor to get us straightened out. After we have exhausted all the human possibilities, we do the thing we should have done in the first place.

So Daniel comes in. There was something about Daniel that kept the king knocking on his door when he got to the end of himself. He said, "I know that the spirit of the holy gods is in you, and no mystery is too difficult for you" (Dan. 4:9). In the truest sense of the Old Testament, Daniel was a spirit-filled man. He was different. Nebuchadnezzar didn't know how to describe him in any other way than his own terminology, and that was the "spirit of the holy gods."

For those who work in the business or professional world, you are going to be criticized and ridiculed because of your faith. Before I became a pastor I worked my way through school in a trucking firm. The other guys called me Preacher Boy and other less endearing terms. But as soon as one of them got into trouble, he came to my truck to talk to me. They knew the guys they caroused with, drank with, and with whom they exchanged dirty jokes didn't have the answers. If we let the spirit of God dwell in us, it won't be long until someone will be knocking at our door. They will see the difference and want some help.

DREAM OF A FEARFUL TREE

When all else fails, read the directions. Nebuchadnezzar finally called in Daniel and asked him to interpret his dream. This one was more unusual than the statue of gold, and it must have put the king into a cold sweat; he even said it terrified him.

In spite of the fact that Daniel had been serving him for thirty years, Nebuchadnezzar called him by his Babylonian name and did not acknowledge the God he had once called "God of gods and the Lord of kings." Daniel's consistent witness was dependable.

The king said:

Here is my dream; interpret it for me. These are the visions I saw while lying in my bed: I looked, and there before me stood a tree in the middle of the land. Its height was enormous. The tree grew large and strong and its top touched the sky; it was visible to the ends of the earth. Its leaves were beautiful, its fruit abundant, and on it was food for all. Under it the beasts of the field found shelter, and the birds of the air lived in its branches; from it every creature was fed.

In the visions I saw while lying in my bed, I looked, and there before me was a messenger, a holy one, coming down from heaven. He called in a loud voice: "Cut down the tree and trim off its branches; strip off its leaves and scatter its fruit. Let the animals flee from under it and the birds from its branches. But let the stump and its roots, bound with iron and bronze, remain in the ground, in the grass of the field.

"Let him be drenched with the dew of heaven, and let him live with the animals among the plants of the earth. Let his mind be changed from that of a man and let him be given the mind of an animal, till seven times pass by for him.

The decision is announced by messengers; the holy ones declare the verdict, so that the living may know that the Most High is sovereign over the kingdoms of men and gives them to anyone he wishes and sets over them the lowliest of men." (Daniel 4:9–17)

The king must have leaned back on his throne and looked at Daniel with pleading eyes. Two parts of this tree frightened him. First, it was a magnificent tree, seen by the whole earth and abundant with fruit, but these messengers (who were angels, representatives from God) came down from heaven and said that the gigantic tree would be cut down and all the birds would fly away from it, and the beasts would no longer take refuge under it. All that was going to be left was a little stump in the ground. The strange thing is that in the beginning of the dream the tree was an "it," but before the end of the description it becomes "him."

The prophecy described in the dream was going to happen over a period of seven years, during which the mind of the man would be changed to the mind of a beast. No one can say this old king had pleasant dreams.

It is quite evident that Daniel loved this reprobate. God had revealed to him the future of his friend, Nebuchadnezzar, through this tragic, terrible dream. As Daniel wrestled with the meaning of the dream, he didn't want to tell the king what he had learned. He was undoubtedly very troubled when he said, "My lord, if only the dream applied to your enemies and its meaning to your adversaries!" (Dan. 4:19).

Daniel gives us a superb pattern of how to preach the judgment of God to people. It needs to be done with a broken heart, with a true concern, pointing out the consequences with mercy. I have a lot of friends in the ministry who can't wait to get to the passages on judgment, because they come on with great vengeance. One thing is missing—the tears.

Years ago in London there was a large gathering of notables for a concert. One of the invited guests was a famous preacher, Caesar Milan. A young lady charmed the audience that night with her singing. After the concert Milan went up to her and graciously, but very boldly, said to her, "I thought as I listened to you tonight how tremendously the cause of Christ would be benefited if your talents were dedicated to His cause. You know, young lady, you are as much a sinner as a drunkard in the ditch . . . in the sight of God, but I'm glad to tell you that the blood of Jesus Christ can cleanse you from all sin."

That lady became so angry at the preacher that she stomped her feet and walked away. As she was leaving he said, "I mean no offense. I pray that God's Spirit will convict you."

Now that's not exactly my style of witnessing, but here's the rest of the story. The young lady went home, but she couldn't sleep. The face of the preacher appeared before her, and his words rang through her mind. About two o'clock in the morning she got out of bed, took a pencil and piece of paper, and with tears rolling down her face, Charlotte Elliot wrote:

> *Just as I am, without one plea,*
> *But that Thy blood was shed for me,*
> *And that Thou bidd'st me come to Thee,*
> *O Lamb of God, I come! I come!*[1]

That song has been sung by choirs throughout the world as an invitation to accept Jesus Christ. Most Billy Graham crusades concluded with it. A few words by a man who preached the judgment of God with a broken heart resulted in tens of thousands of new Christians declaring their faith. I wonder what would happen if that would be our modus operandi in the ministry today.

I WISH I DIDN'T HAVE TO TELL YOU

Truth sometimes hurts. We avoid telling the ones we love of the sin in their lives, knowing that we are living in glass houses ourselves. It must have troubled Daniel deeply to interpret this dream for the king.

> This is the interpretation, O king, and this is the decree the Most High has issued against my lord the king: You will be driven away from people and will live with the wild animals; you will eat grass like cattle and be drenched with the dew of heaven. Seven times will pass by for you until you acknowledge

that the Most High is sovereign over the kingdoms of men and gives them to anyone he wishes. The command to leave the stump of the tree with its roots means that your kingdom will be restored to you when you acknowledge that Heaven rules. (Dan. 4:24–26)

We don't know if Nebuchadnezzar answered Daniel or not; however, we can imagine that he leaned forward, looked Daniel straight in the eyes and thought, *What an improbable idea! I would never grovel on the ground like a wild animal.*

As a man of God, Daniel did not leave the king without a solution. His advice was polite and to the point, "Renounce your sins by doing what is right, and your wickedness by being kind to the oppressed. It may be that then your prosperity will continue" (Dan. 4:27).

God always warns us before He sends judgment. He says, "Listen and obey or suffer the consequences." He sent a voice from heaven as the warning, but He gave the king a chance to turn his life around. I believe that God does that for us today. He tells us, "Look, you're headed for a crash. Turn around or you'll land in a ditch that's so deep you won't be able to pull yourself out."

Nebuchadnezzar was given a year's reprieve, but he refused to repent. For twelve months, while Daniel probably waited and prayed for him, the king ignored the caution signs. Then the day arrived. He was walking on the roof of the royal palace, surveying the magnificent scene below. This was no ordinary roof; this was something of such proportions that our modern walls would look Lilliputian in comparison. According to the ancient historian Herodotus, the walls of Babylon were 320 feet high, which is almost a third of the height of the Empire State Building, and they were 80 feet thick and 56 miles long. (And we think our feats of engineering today are advanced.) Several chariots could be driven on the top of the wall, and one of the great sports was to have races on them. Remember the chariot races in *Ben Hur?* Imagine them going around and around the city, like an elaborate train around a Christmas tree.

The mighty Euphrates River flowed through the midst of the city. On one bank of the river there were abundant terraces that led to a central altar, and in the middle of the city was the huge temple of Bel, with all its temples and palaces. If we had walked around Babylon at that time, we would have been awed by the spacious gardens and orchards that produced enough to feed the whole population.

So Nebuchadnezzar strolled along the wall, probably leading an entourage of his counselors and cabinet, looking over the city with inflated pride, and said, "Is not this the great Babylon I have built as the royal residence, by my mighty power and for the glory of my majesty?" (Dan. 4:30).

One moment he was a bright, handsome, thriving executive king, his mind sharp and clear. The arrogant words were no sooner out of his mouth than like a clap of thunder his mind snapped. The next moment he was reduced to an animal, with the mind of a beast and a form of insanity called monomania, which means that one part of normal human functioning doesn't work while all the rest is operating. Specifically, this is called lycanthropy, which comes from two words: *lycos,* meaning "wolf," and *anthropos,* meaning "man." He was not a Jekyll and Hyde, but a wolf-man.

The once mighty king was so ugly that the people must have been repulsed by his appearance, a creature who ate grass like an animal, covered with slime and scratching his filthy, tangled hair with his clawlike nails.

When Nebuchadnezzar said, "Look at me, world; look what I

have done," God kept His promise and judged him and lowered him to the lowest possible place he could still be alive. He was probably confined by an iron fence, which is the band of metal he saw surrounding the stump in his dream.

Imagine this caged animal growling menacingly as children and adults taunted him or walked by with eyes averted. Who would want to look at such a horrible creature?

In recent times there have been men who have reached important public and financial positions only to fall into the iron cages of jail or disgrace for flaunting the laws of God and society. It is not beyond the power of God to offer restoration.

After seven years of physical and mental torture, Nebuchadnezzar said, "I . . . raised my eyes toward heaven, and my sanity was restored. Then I praised the Most High; I honored and glorified him who lives forever" (Dan. 4:34). What a testimony of praise this is:

> His dominion is an eternal dominion;
> his kingdom endures from generation to generation.
> All the peoples of the earth
> are regarded as nothing.
> He does as he pleases
> with the powers of heaven
> and the peoples of the earth.
> No one can hold back his hand
> or say to him: "What have you done?" (Dan. 4:34–35)

As quickly as he went insane, his sanity was restored. Also, his advisers and nobles sought him out, and his throne was restored to him with even greater power than he had before. But this time he acknowledged where that power came from.

It is almost unbelievable that after seven years, his kingdom was still secure. No foreign power had come and confiscated it; there had been no national uprising or coup to depose him. Perhaps it was Daniel who held things together.

Nebuchadnezzar learned a lasting lesson. "Now I, Nebuchadnezzar, praise and exalt and glorify the King of heaven, because everything he does is right and all his ways are just. And those who walk in pride he is able to humble" (Dan. 4:37).

That is the last we hear about Nebuchadnezzar in the Bible, but I believe we will meet him someday in heaven. The Lord brought him from wickedness to righteousness with a severe lesson in animal husbandry.

PRIDE AND PREJUDICE

Pride is not the sole possession of the powerful, the rich, or the famous. It gets everybody if we're not careful. Of all of the personal and church problems I have seen in my years in the ministry, most of them are the result of pride. If we think that God hasn't dealt with us or others about this problem, or that He is not going to do it, we are quite mistaken. There is a strong statement in Ecclesiastes 8:11: "When the sentence for a crime is not quickly carried out, the hearts of the people are filled with schemes to do wrong." Just because we say we're home free when God doesn't zap us about our wrongdoing doesn't mean that God isn't going to do anything. God sees our hearts, and He gives us warnings, but if we refuse, He will deal with our pride.

Sometimes we feel like we're pawns in some wicked world struggle. We feel helpless when proud and cruel leaders whip the nations into a frenzy of animosities. But we don't have to worry about what God is doing in our generation; "His dominion is an eternal dominion; his kingdom endures from generation to generation" (Dan. 4:34).

Nebuchadnezzar's testimony is a political message for all of our leaders until Christ returns. The message is simple: God rules.

8

YOUR NUMBER IS UP

Seventy years after the Hebrew children were taken captive and carried off to Babylon, one of the best-known drunken brawls in history took place. Babylon the Great met its Waterloo and went down to ignominious defeat. The story has the intrigue of a modern adventure-thriller, but if you had been a super sleuth, you would have discovered that its plot had been divulged many years before by the old prophet Jeremiah.

Jeremiah had a knack for bringing sad tidings of no joy, but his foretelling of events was accurate. He said, "'Before your eyes I will repay Babylon and all who live in Babylonia for all the wrong they have done in Zion,' declares the LORD" (Jer. 51:24). And that is the story you are about to hear.

There was a succession of kings in Babylon after Nebuchadnezzar died. Most of them experienced untimely deaths. One was assassinated by his brother, another was killed in battle, and another was captured by the Medes and the Persians and lived the life of a prisoner of war. Onto the scene comes Belshazzar, a man who was addicted to wine, women, and song, and whose infamous party coined a phrase passed down to us twenty-five centuries later: the handwriting on the wall.

THE FEAST OF BELSHAZZAR

Let's look back to the book of Daniel:

> King Belshazzar gave a great banquet for a thousand of his nobles and drank wine with them. While Belshazzar was drinking his wine, he gave orders to bring in the gold and silver goblets that Nebuchadnezzar his father had taken from the temple in Jerusalem, so that the king and his nobles, his wives and his concubines might drink from them. (Dan. 5:1–2)

Belshazzar was not really Nebuchadnezzar's son, but his grandson. In the language in which this was written, there was no name for grandfather or grandson, so any ancestor was referred to as a father.

Where was our hero at this time? Historians tell us that after Nebuchadnezzar died, all of the ministers who were at the core of the palace regulars were banished and sent away from the throne. Daniel, being one of those ministers, virtually dropped out of sight for almost a decade and lived in obscurity. When Belshazzar sent out invitations to his Debauchery Ball, Daniel was not on the guest list.

The party the king threw was in honor of the Babylonian god Bel. After all, Belshazzar was named for that god, so it would be quite right in his mind to honor Bel with a festival. When archaeologists excavated the site in modern times, they discovered that the huge hall where the party was held was some 60 feet wide and 172 feet long. The entire main section of the White House in Washington, DC, is approximately that size.

Belshazzar sat on his throne above the thousand nobles and their assorted female companions and led them in drinking toasts to their pagan gods. This act in itself was totally beneath the dignity of the kings of that day. If they drank, it was in private, not at public spectacles. Belshazzar flung protocol to the winds and also invited women to his drunken party. This was a real taboo, but he threw all restraints aside and did exactly as he pleased.

Proverbs 31:4–5 says: "It is not for kings, O Lemuel—not for kings to drink wine, not for rulers to crave beer, lest they drink and forget what the law decrees."

Another prophet warned: "Woe to those who are heroes at drinking wine and champions at mixing drinks . . . as dry grass sinks down in the flames, so their roots will decay" (Isa. 5:22–24).

This drunken orgy was accompanied by overtones of sensuality by the presence of the women. The scene was not unlike many of the great parties that go on in our day.

I must admit I've lived a sheltered life. Never in all my experience have I been to a party like that, nor do I intend to go. However, I remember an occasion when I was a student in Texas. Because I sold programs for football games in the Cotton Bowl, I had a ticket to every game. I remember one weekend that gave me a small glimpse into what an intoxicated crowd would do. The game was between two archrival teams. I was working as the head of a custodial crew in downtown Dallas (nice expression for the clean-up gang), and when I went into the streets the night before the game, I couldn't believe my eyes. Men and women, young and old alike, were staggering up and down the street. They literally walked back and forth in a drunken stupor. There was nakedness and immorality and sin, all in the name of a good time. It was a repulsive sight I shall never forget.

Belshazzar also indulged in the worst sacrilege. He sent for the gold and silver goblets that Nebuchadnezzar had taken from the Jerusalem temple and commanded that they be filled with wine for all to drink. In open defiance of those holy vessels, he taunted the Hebrew God with this act of desecration.

We can imagine Belshazzar ordering his slaves to bring in these holy vessels, hidden deep in the vault and never touched by all of the preceding kings, dusting off the grime of the years, and lifting them high to be shown off to the crowd. When the moment came for this scum of a man to begin his toasts, the orchestra stopped playing, the erotic dancers ceased, and Belshazzar, smirking with insolence, slopped the wine down his chin, staining his beard with the crimson liquid. *Look at what I have done. I am the king, I have no fear of a foreign god!* The crowd cheered this daring act and continued their revelry.

Joseph A. Seiss, in his book *Voices from Babylon*, wrote:

Not only their ill-timed merriment, their trampling on the customary proprieties, and their drunkenness, but even their foolhardy and blasphemous insult to the most High God is veiled over and cloaked up with a pretense of devotion. But this was as far as it was possible for human daring and infatuation to go. It was more than the powers of heaven could quietly endure. This was the end.[1]

SACRILEGE AND STUPIDITY

Visualize yourself in church as communion is being served. On the communion table are the little glasses in which the juice is poured, honoring the death of our Lord. Suddenly an inebriated man swerves up the center aisle, grabs a cup from the tray, throws the juice on the floor, and fills it up with a shot of whiskey. He then turns around and shouts to the congregation, "Here's a toast to the devil!"

That is what happened that fateful night in Babylon. Is it any wonder that God said, "Enough is enough. Your number is up!"

Belshazzar was not only grossly sacrilegious, he was also stupid. He was literally celebrating his own funeral, but he didn't know it. Jeremiah, almost a hundred years before, had prophesied in nearly exact detail everything that was going to happen that night.

First, Jeremiah told us that Babylon would be conquered by a nation from the north. His words were so detailed that anyone skeptical about biblical prophecy should be convinced:

This is the word the LORD spoke through Jeremiah the prophet concerning Babylon and the land of the Babylonians:

"Announce and proclaim among the nations,
lift up a banner and proclaim it;
keep nothing back, but say,
Babylon will be captured;
Bel will be put to shame,
Marduk filled with terror.
Her images will be put to shame
and her idols filled with terror.
A nation from the north will attack her
and lay waste her land.
No one will live in it;
both men and animals will flee away." (Jer. 50:1–3)

Remember the statue? After the head of gold, which was Babylon, the next empire to take over was the Medo-Persian. Here's what Jeremiah had to say:

Sharpen the arrows,
take up the shields!
The LORD has stirred up the kings of the Medes,
because his purpose is to destroy Babylon.
The LORD will take vengeance,
vengeance for his temple. (Jer. 51:11)

Prepare the nations for battle against her—
the kings of the Medes,
their governors and all their officials,
and all the countries they rule.
The land trembles and writhes,
for the LORD's purposes against Babylon stand—
to lay waste the land of Babylon
so that no one will live there. (Jer. 51:28–29)

In another passage, Jeremiah told how Babylon was going to be captured and even gave clues about the subterfuge that would cause the city to surrender without a battle.

"I will make her officials and wise men drunk,
her governors, officers and warriors as well;
they will sleep forever and not awake,"
declares the King, whose name is the LORD Almighty. (Jer. 51:57)

As if these prophecies aren't accurate enough, Jeremiah even gave us a few clues on how this military victory would be won.

See, I will defend your cause
and avenge you;

I will dry up her sea
and make her springs dry.
Babylon will be a heap of ruins,
a haunt of jackals,
an object of horror and scorn,
a place where no one lives. (Jer. 51:36–37)

MARK MY WORDS

Jot down Jeremiah's words in your mental notebook, like a participant in a "Solve the Mystery" game, then we'll return to Belshazzar's ball.

Of all the stupid parties in history, this one takes the prize. At the very moment Belshazzar and his guests were becoming more and more inebriated, slopping down their liquor from the holy vessels of the God of Jerusalem, their mortal enemies were coming under the walls of the city.

THE GOPHER MANEUVER

Cyrus was the leader of the Medes and Persians, who were intent on conquering Babylon. The Babylonians had decided to forego the battlefield and fortify themselves within the mighty walls of their city. One historian said that the Babylonians had enough food, water, and provisions to last the entire city for more than twenty years.

When Cyrus besieged the city, he realized he couldn't do this forever, so he devised another plan. The great Euphrates River ran under the wall and through the city, so Cyrus took the best men of his army and stationed half of them at the place where the river entered the city and the other half where it ran out. Then he took the rest of his army and went to a place where the Euphrates passed a huge swamp. He built a huge sluice gate or canal by which he diverted the Euphrates away from the city.

Cyrus ordered the soldiers at the front and the back of the city to watch the river, and once the water receded, they were directed to march into the city without being observed. What an ingenious plan!

As the water level began to recede, the soldiers tested the height of the river until they were able to stand up. Then, one after another, from both ends, without even being seen, the entire army began to breach this impregnable city. Babylon was the city they thought could never be taken, but it was.

THE GHOSTLY FINGER

Back to the party:

> Suddenly the fingers of a human hand appeared and wrote on the plaster of the wall, near the lampstand in the royal palace. The king watched the hand as it wrote. His face turned pale and he was so frightened his knees knocked together and his legs gave way. (Dan. 5:5–6)

Belshazzar must have set the all-time record for sobriety. Gone was the smirk, the defiance of God; instead he had a look of stark terror. He became so weak that he couldn't stand up or sit down. In one brief moment, the profane king became a shivering, shaking, helpless mortal. So what did he do? He shrieked for the same old crowd—the enchanters, astrologers, and diviners. If they were at the party, they must have sobered up pretty fast too. They were true to their reputation; they couldn't read the handwriting on the wall, nor could they interpret what it meant.

While the king and his nobles were moaning and cowering in fear at the mysterious handwriting, the queen mother, who undoubtedly lived in an apartment somewhere in the palace, heard the ruckus and came into the banquet hall to find out what had happened. This woman was probably Nebuchadnezzar's wife, who had watched her famous husband groveling like an animal for seven years and then be restored to his throne when he believed in the one God. She had not attended the party, but when she did arrive she had some excellent advice. She remembered Daniel and began to recall for Belshazzar the ministry of this man whom she said had a "keen mind and knowledge and understanding, and also the ability to interpret dreams, explain riddles and solve difficult problems" (Dan. 5:12).

It seems evident by her words that Daniel was not then at the core of the Babylonian government, certainly not under Belshazzar as he had been under Nebuchadnezzar. He must have been assigned to some lower echelon. It was quite probable when Belshazzar came into power as nothing more than a drunken, spoiled brat, he surmised that having Daniel around wouldn't be very advantageous to his kingdom. However, the queen mother knew the influence Daniel had on her husband and that he was still alive and well somewhere in the area. Although Daniel was eighty years old, he was the only hope in the kingdom for interpreting what was written on the wall that night.

Belshazzar called for Daniel. Waiting for him to arrive must have been agonizing; the music had stopped, the revelry was over, and all the nobles and their assorted women were milling around, trying to clear their befuddled minds. When Daniel was brought in, the king steadied himself and said, "Are you Daniel, one of the exiles my father the king brought from Judah? I have heard that the spirit of the gods is in you and that you have insight, intelligence and outstanding wisdom" (Dan. 5:13–14)

Then Belshazzar offered Daniel a bribe: "If you can read this writing and tell me what it means, you will be clothed in purple and have a gold chain placed around your neck, and you will be made the third highest ruler in the kingdom" (Dan. 5:16).

Isn't it interesting that Daniel wasn't present at the time when he was needed? Remember he wasn't present when Nebuchadnezzar had his first dream, and he wasn't there when Nebuchadnezzar had his second dream. This time he wasn't around when God wrote on the wall. He was not there when the humanist pagan counselors were called to give their interpretation. He was always by himself, away from the drunkenness, the partying, and the humanists. As a last resort Daniel was called.

An English preacher by the name of Joseph Parker had a good word for all of us preachers on this passage. He said:

Preachers of the Word, you will be wanted someday by Belshazzar. You were not at the beginning of the feast. You will be there before the banquet hour is closed. The king will not ask you to drink wine, but he will ask you to tell the secret of his pain, and heal the malady of his heart. Just wait your time, preachers. You are nobody now. Who cares for preachers and teachers and seers, men of insight, while the wine goes around and the feast is unfolding its tempting luxuries. But the preacher will have his opportunity. They will send for him when all other friends have failed. May he then come fearlessly, independently, asking only to be a channel through which divine communication can be addressed. Then may he speak to the listening trouble of the world.[2]

That's encouraging for preachers. We don't get a very good press. In fact, in a list of the most important professions we are conspicuously absent. Television lumps us in a heap with the charlatans, and the movies seldom bother to acknowledge that we exist. Someday, in the prologue to the Tribulation, when things start to heat up more than they are, we are going to see the churches where Bible-teaching pastors preach the Word of God in places jammed to the rafters with people who will come to hear what God has to say.

POSITION, POSSESSIONS, AND POWER

Daniel was the king's last resort. He said, "Look, I brought in my brain trust and asked them this question, but they didn't know anything." Today the secular wise men cannot know the things of the Spirit of God, but when advice is asked, that's where the world goes.

Belshazzar used the only motivation he knew to give, the enticement of position, possessions, and power. "Look, Daniel, here's everything a man could ever want, just tell me what to do about those words."

"Then Daniel answered the king, 'You may keep your gifts for yourself and give your rewards to someone else. Nevertheless, I will read the writing for the king and tell him what it means'" (Dan. 5:17).

Daniel doesn't have a word of sympathy for the king. He doesn't have anything good to say about this reprobate. When he was involved with Nebuchadnezzar, he came to like him, but he had no love for Belshazzar. Why the difference? Because Belshazzar profaned the holiness of Daniel's God by drinking to his pagan gods with the vessels that belonged to the holy God.

Daniel's voice, his words, and his composed manner were in accord with the Spirit who wrote those awful words on the wall. The prophet knew that he was about to utter some of the last words the royal sinner would ever hear in his life.

Daniel was a man who would not take a bribe or even be enticed by a reward. He told the king to keep his stuff. Although he respected

Nebuchadnezzar, he rejected Belshazzar. He was like Abraham who told the king of Sodom that he wouldn't even take a shoelace from him (Gen. 14:22–23). The apostle Paul said, "I have not coveted anyone's silver or gold or clothing" (Acts 20:33).

After Daniel refused the gifts, he reviewed the king's heritage and history. He reminded him of how Nebuchadnezzar had been reduced to an animal until he finally acknowledged the Most High God. The purpose of reciting history in an introduction to his sermon was to help Belshazzar see himself in the same place as Nebuchadnezzar in relation to God. We can imagine the shivering king thinking, *Get on with it, old man. I don't need a sermon, I need an interpretation.*

PREMEDITATED SIN

Most sermons from our pulpits today are milquetoast renditions compared to those given by the holy men of the Bible. Daniel told it like it was.

> But you his son, O Belshazzar, have not humbled yourself, though you knew all this. Instead, you have set yourself up against the Lord of heaven. You had the goblets from his temple brought to you, and you and your nobles, your wives and your concubines drank wine from them. You praised the gods of silver and gold, of bronze, iron, wood and stone, which cannot see or hear or understand. But you did not honor the God who holds in his hand your life and all your ways. Therefore he sent the hand that wrote the inscription. (Dan. 5:22–24)

Not only did Daniel charge the king with premeditated sin and profane sacrilege, but also with pagan sacrifice. He told him, in front of the whole motley bunch of court followers, "Belshazzar, you are a fool! You have taken God's holy vessels and lifted them up to praise false gods."

God "holds in his hand your life and all your ways." Job said, "In his hand is the life of every creature and the breath of all mankind" (Job 12:10). We breathe so naturally and never think about it, but the day God decides He doesn't want us to breathe any longer, it's all over. Our breath is in His hand. Many people use the breath He gave them to curse His name. How foolish it is for any of God's creatures to mock the Creator who is in charge!

THE HANDWRITING EXPERT

Across those whitewashed walls were sprawled these words in Aramaic: "MENE, MENE, TEKEL, PARSIN." The meaning of that phrase seals the fate of Babylon.

Mene: God has numbered the days of your reign and brought it to an end.

It's all over, Belshazzar; God has called your number. Behind the magnificent walls of Babylon, the king laughed at the approach of Cyrus, but that night the Medo-Persian armies were creeping in under the city, ready for the kill.

Tekel: You have been weighed on the scales and found wanting.

That meant that the kingdom had been weighed and found to be too light, lacking in value. Babylon failed to meet God's standard. The ancient Egyptians had a true idea of this divine judgment, although it was misapplied to their pagan god, Osiris. They said that after death, a person was taken to the hall of judgment where his heart was removed and weighed on the scales against a feather. If the heart was light, he was pure. If not, he was weighted down with sin and would suffer punishment. That pagan theology was close to the truth.

The Bible says that God weighs us in His balance. "Let God weigh me in honest scales and he will know that I am blameless" (Job 31:6). "Do not keep talking so proudly or let your mouth speak such arrogance, for the LORD is a God who knows, and by him deeds are weighed" (1 Sam. 2:3). When we talk about judgment being a "weighty matter," it is truly God who holds the balance scales.

Peres: Your kingdom is divided and given to the Medes and Persians.

That night, when God looked down and saw the drunken orgy, He extended His hand and wrote on the wall, saying, "MENE, MENE, [your number's up] TEKEL [you have been weighed and found wanting], PARSIN [your kingdom is divided and given to the Medes and the Persians]." It was all over.

BABYLON, O BABYLON

Belshazzar didn't seem to get the message immediately, because he ordered Daniel to be clothed in royal robes with a gold chain around his neck and to be proclaimed the third-highest ruler in the kingdom. Daniel had told him he wasn't interested in that stuff; he knew these honors would be short-lived and useless.

"That very night Belshazzar, king of the Babylonians, was

YOUR NUMBER IS UP

slain, and Darius the Mede took over the kingdom, at the age of sixty-two" (Dan. 5:30).

That night, according to historians, was the sixteenth day of Tishri 539 BC, about October 11 or 12 on our calendar. Babylon collapsed, joining the host of nations that have forgotten God and have fallen, going back as far as the Hittites, the Egyptians, and the Assyrians. Isaiah the prophet said, "Surely the nations are like a drop in a bucket; they are regarded as dust on the scales" (Isa. 40:15).

ARE WE LIKE DUST?

Although it seems like we read about more and more government scandals every week, I don't believe we know half the truth of the Belshazzars who party in our state and national capitals. We look at the wonderful achievements of America and say, "Look at this great Babylon in which we live."

That prophetic handwriting has an application to our time. The Bible says:

> But mark this: There will be terrible times in the last days. People will be lovers of themselves, lovers of money, boastful, proud, abusive, disobedient to their parents, ungrateful, unholy, without love, unforgiving, slanderous, without self-control, brutal, not lovers of the good, treacherous, rash, conceited, lovers of pleasure rather than lovers of God—having a form of godliness but denying its power. (2 Tim. 3:1–5)

It was curtains for Belshazzar when he took the holy vessels of God and desecrated them. What about us? We don't have personal access to the ancient cups of gold. But the Bible says our bodies are temples of the Lord, the vessels of God. When we take holy things that belong to God and corrupt them with drugs, alcohol, and the degrading things of the world, God's judgment is soon at the door. That's a pretty sobering thought.

Just as the downfall of Babylon meant the end of a great civilization, so the end of the age will be marked by the extinction of the Gentile world powers. The doom of Babylon foreshadows the doom of Babylon the Great, the mother of harlots (Rev. 17:5). People today laugh when we tell them that our modern civilization is doomed, but I'm certain that Belshazzar never conceived in his mind that his mighty empire would be overthrown.

Let's considered the lyrics hymnist Knowles Shaw wrote in 1877 for his hymn "The Handwriting on the Wall":

> At the feast of Belshazzar
> And a thousand of his lords,
> While they drank from golden vessels,
> As the Book of Truth records,
> In the night as they reveled
> In the royal palace hall,
> They were seized with consternation
> At the hand upon the wall.
> So our deeds are recorded,
> There's a Hand that's writing now.
> Sinner, give your heart to Jesus
> To His royal mandate bow.
> For the day is approaching,
> It must come to one and all,
> When the sinner's condemnation
> Will be written on the wall.[3]

This is not fiction. The Bible has spelled this out for many centuries, but it is only with the increasing signs of the end of the age that prophetic truth has quickened the hearts of believers, as it has mine.

9

POLITICAL
INTRIGUE

It was an election year. The pundits and commentators had their spears sharpened to mortally wound one prominent candidate. They conspired in secluded locations and hired the best investigators; they practiced innuendoes and slanted reports. Unknown sources were quoted, and an important government official told the press corps that this candidate took his religious beliefs into his governmental duties. He was not politically correct.

In a private, carefully guarded room of the Median palace in Babylon, the governors of more than a hundred provinces gathered secretly. *The king plans to put this Daniel as head over the whole kingdom. He's got to go or we don't have a chance with our own plans. We need to discredit him first in the eyes of the king and destroy him in the process.* The heads of states pulled their beards and shook their heads. They had not been able to bring any charges against their opponent. He wasn't a womanizer. He didn't have any vested interests in a Persian Savings and Loan. And he had too many friends in high places. Even Darius the Mede, whom Cyrus had put in charge of the conquered Babylonian territories, favored him.

They checked all of the things he had done, every single memo he had ever written. They dogged him, bugged his rooms, and had the Medo-Persian FBI follow every lead. They were burning with rage and envy.

Finally, one of the conspirators came up with a brilliant idea. "We will never find any basis for charges against this man Daniel unless it has something to do with the law of his God" (Dan. 6:5).

The governors broke into applause and congratulated each other on this skillful maneuver. If the usual tactics of political subterfuge didn't work, this would certainly seal the fate of this infidel. They sent a special messenger to the palace and requested an audience with the king.

CORRUPTION IN THE KINGDOM

Why did all of those people want Daniel's neck? If we look at the vast empire under Darius, it was much like modern government. The 120 princes were ripping off the king. Darius was no fool. He knew the princes were withholding money that they collected from taxation and that they were using it for themselves and costly government programs. He knew Daniel's reputation and decided to put him at the top of this flow chart, hoping he could cut out the graft. No wonder Daniel was hated by the extortioners who had their Rolls Royce chariots and Riviera vacations courtesy of the taxpayers.

Jealousy reared its ugliest head. Someone said that jealousy is the tribute that mediocrity pays to genius. The greatest tribute to Daniel was the fact that those who worked with him knew what he was and tried in every way to get rid of him.

We sometimes think that our biblical heroes lived in an unreal world, that we could never relate to them. Alexander McClaren expressed the reality of Daniel's world:

It's remarkable that a character of such beauty and consecration as Daniel's should be rooted and grow out of the court where Daniel was. For this court was half shambles and half pigsty. It was filled with luxury and sensuality and lust and self-seeking and idolatry and ruthless cruelty. And in the middle of this there grew up that fair flower of character, pure and stainless by the acknowledgement of his enemies.[1]

There's always a price to be paid for leadership, in any field. The musician, the athlete, the man or woman who gives himself to excellence will sooner or later pay the price of primacy. A person who has been blessed by God with some small success always pays a penalty for what he has done.

MEANWHILE, BACK AT THE PALACE

There was confusion inside the throne room. The governors trooped in, all talking noisily and catching the king off guard. First of all, they began with a lie. They stated that all the leaders in the kingdom had consulted together, and yet they knew that Daniel was never involved. Next, they used flattery to get the king's attention. They rushed into his presence and said, "Your highness, we've been thinking, and we've decided we are going to make you god for a month."

They bowed before the king and with inward smugness said:

O King Darius, live forever! The royal administrators, prefects, satraps, advisers and governors have all agreed that the king should issue an edict and enforce the decree that anyone who prays to any god or man during the next thirty days, except to you, O king, shall be thrown into the lions' den. Now, O king, issue the decree and put it in writing so that it cannot be altered—in accordance with the laws of the Medes and Persians, which cannot be repealed. (Dan. 6:6–8)

Darius thought that sounded pretty good. In Proverbs 27:4 (KJV) it says, "Wrath is cruel, and anger is outrageous; but who is able to stand before envy?" These men were so filled with envy they tricked their own king into signing something they knew in their hearts he didn't want to sign. This carefully strategized plot was built upon the vanity of the king.

Darius signed the decree, which was established according to the law of the Medes and the Persians. In that culture, they believed their monarchs were infallible; therefore, they could never make a mistake. The king himself could not change what he had written, because that would be admitting his fallibility, so the law of the Medes and the Persians came to be a law that could never be changed. Darius put the decree in writing, and he was stuck with it.

When Daniel heard about the decree, he went home and did exactly what he was accustomed to doing. He got down on his knees and prayed. "He went home to his upstairs room where the windows opened toward Jerusalem. Three times a day he got down on his knees and prayed, giving thanks to his God, just as he had done before" (Dan. 6:10). Daniel was like David in this respect. In Psalm 55:17, we read of David, "Evening, morning and noon I cry out in distress, and he hears my voice." The exciting thing about Daniel is that he didn't change when the pressure was on. I believe that is one of the greatest characteristics of godliness in people's lives—they can move through the vicissitudes of life, untouched by the circumstances, because of the consistency of their example and the godliness of their walk.

Psalm 46:1–2 says:

> God is our refuge and strength,
> an ever-present help in trouble.
> Therefore we will not fear, though the earth give way
> and the mountains fall into the heart of the sea.

That's it. No matter what happens, just go forward.

Daniel probably had a prayer chamber on the top level of his house where he prayed while he faced Jerusalem. It was an act of faith on the part of an exiled Jew to pray toward the land from which he had been taken captive. It was a way to say by one's very posture, "God, I believe Your promise that You will someday return us to our land." In spite of the decree banning all prayer except to Darius, Daniel quietly carried on his activity.

Like the super sleuth who hides in the bushes or who lingers across the street by the lamppost, the jealous politicians watched Daniel praying. They hurried back to the palace and said, with all piety and aplomb:

> "Did you not publish a decree that during the next thirty days anyone who prays to any god or man except to you, O king, would be thrown into the lions' den?"
> The king answered, "The decree stands—in accordance with the laws of the Medes and Persians, which cannot be repealed." (Dan. 6:12)

We've snared him now, the informers smirked to themselves. *Daniel's goose is cooked. The king doesn't dare reverse his order. The lions will have a tasty feast tonight!* And so they told the king about Daniel's praying.

Darius was "greatly distressed" because he truly respected Daniel, and he "made every effort until sundown to save him" (Dan. 6:14). But the trap had been sprung. Daniel and the king were both caught in it, and there wasn't anything that could be done.

THIS DANIEL: UNREAL OR UNAFFECTED?

Someone said to me, "This guy Daniel is unreal. You talk about a guy who couldn't be caught doing anything wrong, a perfect record. And you think we could be like him? Come on, now."

The more I study about him, the more there is a desire in my heart to be like Daniel. What was the basis of his greatness? I believe there are four contributing qualities in Daniel's makeup.

First, Daniel had a *consistent attitude.* The Scripture says he had an excellent spirit, which is how the queen mother described him to Belshazzar. In other words, he had a good attitude. Someone once told me that our attitudes determine our altitude; how far are you going to go? There are a lot of Christians who have bad attitudes. They're whiners and complainers. I don't like to be around them—they discourage me.

Daniel was a positive guy. He moved through all the debris of his generation and never let it get to him. He was always excited about the right things.

Second, Daniel was *consistent in his performance.* He was a man who took his assignments seriously. If he was scheduled to do something, you didn't have to worry about it getting done. He was a man God used because he was trustworthy; you could believe in him. He had credibility. How we need people like that in our lives—people who will give us their word and we can count on them to do what they say they will do.

Also, Daniel had not only a consistent posture and a consistent performance, but he had a *consistent purity*. The highest government officials of the land were determined to peek into every dark corner of his life, but they couldn't find one accusation to lay against him for all of his eighty-some years.

One day some people came to see Charles Haddon Spurgeon, one of the finest preachers in the world. They were trying to blackmail him. They walked into his office and threatened him, saying that if he didn't stop preaching against certain sins, they would publish things that would ruin his reputation. He responded by inviting them to go ahead with their demands—to write everything they knew about him across the heavens.[2]

Now that's the power of a clear conscience.

I heard about a man who went into a fast-food place to get some fried chicken. He had a woman in his car, and they were going to have a picnic at the beach. He bought his chicken, but when they got to the beach he opened the box and found to his surprise that it was full of money. The receipts for the day's business were in the box. The manager had used the carton as a cashbox in order to camouflage it when he took it to the bank. Somehow he had mixed the boxes. The man knew he had to return the money, so he took the box back to the restaurant. Handing it over to the startled manager, he said, "You know this isn't our money. Obviously, there has been some mistake, and I just wanted to get it back to you."

The manager was dumbfounded by the whole thing and said, "Look, this sort of thing never gets reported in the newspapers. I'm going to phone a reporter right now and have him get this story."

The man said, "Wait, please don't do that."

"Why not? What do you mean?"

"Well," he said sheepishly, "you see, the woman in the car isn't my wife."

This is the kind of purity we have in our generation, even among some Christians. We say we're living godly lives, but under the surface is a cesspool.

Daniel was not just a prayer warrior, he was a prayer general. Prayer was a habit with him in spite of the fact that he was a very busy man. He was the prime minister of Medo-Persia, and just trying to stay a jump ahead of those corrupt governors and princes would have to be a full-time job. But he took time to pray three times a day because it was a priority.

There's a slogan I've seen on some walls that says, "If you are really having a busy day, skip your devotions. Signed, Satan."

Daniel was so extreme about his praying that he got on his knees to pray. There's a church in Texas where I have spoken, and it made a deep impression on me. They have kneeling benches, and they pray on their knees. The whole staff prays on their knees, and when they have a public prayer, they walk up to the front of the sanctuary and get down on their knees.

I don't want to start a controversy about a body's position in prayer, but a little poem by Sam Walter Foss describes how we ought to pray:

> The proper way for a man to pray,
> Says Deacon Lemuel Keys,
> And the only proper attitude
> Is down upon his knees.
>
> No, I should say the way to pray,
> Says Reverend Doctor Wise

Is standing straight with outstretched arms
And rapt and upturned eyes.

Oh, no, no, no, said Elmer Slow.
Such posture is too proud.
A man should pray with eyes fast closed
And head contritely bowed.

It seems to me his hands should be
Austerely clasped in front.
Both hands pointing toward the ground,
Said Reverend Doctor Blunt.

Last year I fell in Hitchkins' well,
Head first, said Cyrus Brown.
And both my heels were stickin' up,
And my head was pointing down.

And I made a prayer right then and there,
The best prayer I ever said.
The prayin'est prayer I ever prayed
Was standin' on my head.[3]

God hears us, even if we're standing on our heads.

DANIEL'S ONE-LINER

The key to Daniel's life is contained in one verse that is profound in its simplicity. The last verse of chapter 1 states, "And Daniel continued . . ." (KJV). No matter what his age, from teenager to senior citizen, Daniel continued constantly. Can you imagine what could happen if we developed such consistency in our lives that the enthusiasm and determination to follow the Lord developed and deepened, grew and blossomed so that from youth to old age we were always a valuable tool in the hand of God? That's what I covet for my life. I want God to so mold and make me that as I grow older, I get better. I don't want to be an angry, contentious, bitter old man.

However, I hope that I will never become a zookeeper and land in the predicament that Daniel did. My hometown has one of the most famous zoos in the world, and believe me, I've seen those big cats at feeding time; I hope that the Lord never orders me to jump over one of those moats and offer my body as cat food.

The next episode in Daniel's life is so familiar that most five-year-olds could repeat it, but it has more drama than any adventure writer could create.

10

THE GREAT RESCUE

The king was snared in a trap of his own making, like a hunter who stepped into his own net. He had to issue the decree to throw Daniel to the lions when the final moment for Daniel's physical salvation was gone. The countdown had reached zero hour, and there was no opportunity for redress or appeals. King Darius ordered the execution at sundown.

When the guards came to get Daniel, he probably went compliantly, not fighting and shouting, "I'm innocent; I haven't done anything wrong." We aren't told of his attitude upon arrest, but his character hadn't changed. It reminds me of Shakespeare's famous line spoken by Caesar, "Cowards die many times before their deaths; The valiant never taste of death but once."[1]

Darius was a mental wreck, and he said to Daniel, "May your God, whom you serve continually, rescue you!" (Dan. 6:16). Then the king went back to the palace and had a wretched, sleepless night, agonizing over his fatal order. The Bible says Darius could not be diverted from his misery. Neither music, nor dancing women, nor food could soothe his troubled heart. Daniel had been in charge of the whole empire, so the king was not only losing a friend, but also his number-one administrator.

"A stone was brought and placed over the mouth of the den, and the king sealed it with his own signet ring and with the rings of his nobles, so that Daniel's situation might not be changed" (Dan. 6:17). With that, the enemies of Daniel thought his fate was sealed.

Only our imaginations can take us into that den. We find out later there weren't kittens down there, because of what eventually happened to Daniel's accusers. When the guards slammed the door shut on the opening and affixed the seal, Daniel slid to the floor of the den. With an ear-shattering roar, the huge cats came bounding from their caverns and skidded to a stop as if a powerful hand had reined them abruptly. Their roars began to fade as they formed a solid wall of fur around this alien intruder, some sniffing at his feet and others gradually nuzzling his side. Others turned with an indifferent snort and ambled back to their caverns.

Daniel slumped down, completely exhausted after his nerve-wracking experience, and prayed a prayer of thanksgiving to Jehovah for his deliverance. He leaned back against the wall to make himself comfortable for the night, but the dungeon was damp and chilly. Two lion cubs moved in his direction, not crouching for an attack, but with obvious friendliness. They nestled close to him, providing him with warmth, cushioning his body in their soft fur. An old lioness crept over and lay in front of him; he stroked their backs and they licked his hand. Soon the head of the old patriarch was pillowed by one of the cubs, and the four slept soundly in perfect peace and tranquility. But poor Darius tossed and turned on his comfortable bed, wracked with guilt and fear. Early the next morning we are rushed into the next scene.

At the first light of dawn, the king got up and hurried to the lions' den. When he came near the den, he called to Daniel in an anguished voice, "Daniel, servant of the living God, has your God, whom you serve continually, been able to rescue you from the lions?" (Dan. 6:19)

Darius was just like many of us; he handed out all of those pious statements about God's saving Daniel, but he obviously didn't believe them. Daniel answered him respectfully, which is quite an accomplishment, considering that Darius had put out a contract for his murder. "O king, live forever! My God sent his angel, and he shut the mouths of the lions. They have not hurt me, because I was found innocent in his sight. Nor have I ever done any wrong before you, O king" (Dan. 6:21–22).

Spurgeon once said that it was a good thing the lions didn't try to eat Daniel. They never would have enjoyed him, because he was 50 percent grit and 50 percent backbone.

Darius was a happy king when he heard the firm voice of Daniel echoing up from the den. He ordered a rope to be dropped through the opening, and Daniel was pulled out of the pit. "No wound was found on him, because he had trusted in his God" (Dan. 6:23).

Now Daniel wasn't any different from you or me, except in the measure of his faith in his almighty God. The history of what God has done in a miraculous way from the beginning of Christianity right up to the modern day is contained in what God does for somebody who believes in Him.

The great Hall of Faith chapter, Hebrews 11, tells us what happens in the life of those who believe in the Lord. Enoch believed in God, and he was taken to heaven without seeing death. Abel offered a more excellent sacrifice than Cain because he believed in his God. Noah built an ark and saved himself and his family because he believed in his God. Abraham went out not knowing where he was going because he believed in his God. Joseph gave a commandment concerning his bones because he believed in his God. Moses refused to be called the son of Pharaoh's daughter, choosing rather to suffer affliction with the people of God, because he believed in his God.

Was Daniel afraid? I believe he must have felt pretty shaky when he was unceremoniously dropped into lion country. A teacher once asked a Sunday school class if they thought Daniel was afraid, and one little girl answered, "I don't think he was scared, 'cause one of the lions was the Lion of the tribe of Judah who was in there with him." That child knew her Bible.

> At the king's command, the men who had falsely accused Daniel were brought in and thrown into the lions' den, along with their wives and children. And before they reached the floor of the den, the lions overpowered them and crushed all their bones. (Dan. 6:24)

There's no doubt about the ferocity of those beasts. They attacked that crowd and devoured them before they hit the ground. Instead of one tough old Jew, they got a lot of tender, spineless Persians for breakfast.

"He who digs a hole and scoops it out falls into the pit he has made" (Ps. 7:15). I believe God often has people fall into the pit when they attempt to harm His anointed ones.

THE "SO WHAT" SYNDROME

Many of us have been hearing this story since we were little kids in Sunday school. We know all of the flannelgraph positions by heart and have worn down crayons coloring it in our coloring books. So what difference does it make to us?

There's not a thing in the book of Daniel that doesn't have a practical application to our lives. The most familiar stories align with situations we face each day.

First, we are wrapped up in the probability of the lions' den. The nature of the Christian faith marks all of us for the lions, because we are out of step with the world around us. Remember that Shadrach, Meshach, and Abednego were standing when everyone else was kneeling. Daniel was kneeling when everyone else was standing. God didn't withhold them from the pressure of certain death; He took them through the fiery furnace and the lions' den.

What are the lions in your life? Perhaps the lions we confront are illness, or business reverses, or slander, or domestic friction. Sooner or later it is inevitable that every single person will face the lions. The Bible says, "Be self-controlled and alert. Your enemy the devil prowls around like a roaring lion looking for someone to devour" (1 Pet. 5:8). But God promises that he will keep us safe in the midst of the lions. "The angel of the LORD encamps around those who fear him, and he delivers them. . . . The lions may grow weak and hungry, but those who seek the LORD lack no good thing" (Ps. 34:7, 10).

When I first began to travel, I would get on an airplane to go somewhere and have a real battle in my soul. I was afraid that something would happen to me and I would never see my family again. What would happen to them while I was gone? In those early days when I went out to speak, I would be tortured in my mind. I would get there and call my wife to see if everything was all right. Then I would go off to preach about trusting God and having faith.

One day I read something that impressed me so profoundly that I haven't worried since then. It said: "A man of God in the will of

God is immortal until his work on earth is done." What that meant to me was that as long as I am a man of God doing the will of God, nothing can touch me until God is done with me. When He's done with me, I don't want to be around anymore.

Now I can get on that plane and trust Him with my family and my safety. If I am in the will of God, going where God wants me to go, I can be sure that God knows what He is doing with me. The promise of the lions' den is this:

> Sometimes the lions' mouths are shut;
> Sometimes God bids us fight or fly;
> Sometimes He feeds us by the brook;
> Sometimes the flowing stream runs dry.
> The danger that His love allows,
> Is safer than our fears may know;
> The peril that His care permits
> Is our defense where'er we go.[2]

WHY DOES GOD . . . ?

The most commonly asked question to and by Christians is, "Why does God let bad things happen?" Why do two innocent men go to prison for several years for a crime neither committed? Why does a child drown in the fishpond at his grandmother's house? Why does the person who gives the most to his church and charities lose his business? Why does the mother of three small children get cancer? Those are real questions asked by people we know. Look at our friend Daniel. Why should he be the one to be thrown to the lions? Is he the hero of this story? Actually he is just one of the supporting actors in this great drama. The real star of the story is God himself.

God sent His angel to deliver Daniel. And King Darius issued a decree, giving glory not to his friend Daniel, but to "the God of Daniel":

> For he is the living God
> and he endures forever;
> his kingdom will not be destroyed,
> his dominion will never end.
> He rescues and he saves;
> he performs signs and wonders
> in the heavens and on the earth.
> He has rescued Daniel
> from the power of the lions. (Dan. 6:26–27)

Can you imagine a decree like that coming from the White House and broadcast over every television station and headlined in every newspaper? That national statement of faith was recorded by a pagan Medo-Persian.

The real focus of the story is on God. He took the lions' den and used it for His own glory and His own purpose, and when the story was all over and written, the purpose of those difficulties was to glorify God.

At the beginning of the sixth chapter of Daniel we had a new regime. At the end of the chapter there is a new religion, all by the decree of a king who was touched by the power of the almighty God.

Why do bad things happen to good people? It is so God might be glorified through our lions'-den experiences. I don't know how He is going to do it, but whenever God asks one of His people to go through difficult times, it is always for the purpose of glorifying Himself, not only in the experience, but in response to that experience.

SO DANIEL PROSPERED

God is the great encourager. After all he went through, the Bible records, "So Daniel prospered during the reign of Darius and the reign of Cyrus the Persian" (Dan. 6:28).

In James 1:12 it says, "Blessed is the man who perseveres under trial, because when he has stood the test, he will receive the crown of life that God has promised to those who love him." The purpose of testing is to glorify God, but it is also to purify us. Whenever we are purified, we prosper; when God puts us in the furnace and He drains off all the dross, we come out as pure gold. Then it's time for a promotion in the plan of God.

During the course of his life, the author of *Pilgrim's Progress*, John Bunyan, was imprisoned under Charles II. If Bunyan had been willing to sign a statement that he would not preach in public, he would have been released from prison. He was incarcerated for twelve years, but he could have been paroled any day if he would agree to the terms. During those twelve years, he had a dependent wife and little children. One of his daughters was a little girl by the name of Mary, and she was blind. In the dungeon, Bunyan often thought of his poor little Mary, and his heart would almost break.

On one occasion, he wrote, "O the thoughts of the hardships I thought my blind one might go under, would break my heart to pieces. Poor child, thought I, what sorrow must thou have for thy portion in this world?" Bunyan remained in the dungeon, and he gave all his concerns, blind Mary included, to the keeping of God. It was toward the end of his imprisonment that he wrote that glorious passage, "If nothing will do unless I make of my conscience a continual butchery and slaughtershop, unless putting out my own eyes, I commit me to the blind to lead me, as I doubt not is desired by some, I have determined, the Almighty God being my help and shield, yet to suffer, if frail life might continue so long, even till the moss shall grow on mine eyebrows, rather than thus to violate my faith and principles."[3]

WHERE HAVE ALL OUR HEROES GONE?

Where are the people who recognize that life is not important if the only thing they value is physical safety and well-being? May our faith be built upon the likes of Daniel and John Bunyan and others who saw the principles of obedience to God as the highest commitment a person could ever make in this life.

Daniel was a committed man, a man of unwavering testimony and faith in his God. When God touched Daniel, He entrusted him with some of the greatest secrets of the ages. It is with great awe that I realize those secrets have been passed on to us to understand, if we have the curiosity to find them out.

11

GOD'S INCREDIBLE PLAN FOR THE NATIONS

You've just settled into your favorite chair with the newest best-seller, a compelling adventure tale. It is so gripping that you've propped your eyes open to turn the pages. Now you've reached the place in the story where the tension is building. The chapter ends, leaving you in agonizing suspense. With weary persistence, you start the next chapter—only to discover that the scene changes to a flashback in time. *Why does the author do this to me? Doesn't he know I need my sleep?*

When Daniel left his furry friends, we don't follow him down the streets of Babylon to his next adventure. Instead, we are transported back to the first year of the reign of Belshazzar. In one of the most profound dream sequences in the Bible, Daniel tells of his troubling visions. The same man who kept his quiet confidence in the face of dictators and wild beasts trembled and turned pale with the knowledge that was revealed to him. The great interpreter could not explain his own dreams but required the services of an angel.

BACK TO THE FUTURE

Dr. John Walvoord, former president of Dallas Seminary and a noted prophetic scholar, said, "The vision of Daniel provides the most comprehensive and detailed prophecy of future events to be found anywhere in the Old Testament."[1]

I am told that among the scribes who copied the Old Testament, the seventh chapter of Daniel was considered the greatest chapter in the Scriptures. This is about pure future prophecy, the record of God's incredible and unchanging plan for the nations. All of our modern futurists who sit in the think tanks of the nations can project their warnings about holes in the ozone, depletion of natural resources, and misuse of nuclear capabilities, but they are unable to give us a clue to the ultimate future of mankind. Daniel does. Anyone who does not believe in a supernatural Bible has a tremendous problem with the truth in this chapter.

The first six chapters of Daniel are history; chapters 7 through 12 are prophecy. Daniel had four major prophetic dreams that took place over a period of about twenty-two years. Chapter 2 of Daniel, where the dream was given to Nebuchadnezzar and interpreted by Daniel, and chapter 7, where the dream is given to Daniel and interpreted by an angel, are placed together in historical perspective. Chapter 2 shows history from a pagan king's viewpoint, with the gigantic statue and a head of gold, chest and arms of silver, belly and thighs of bronze, legs of iron, and feet of iron and clay. That was Nebuchadnezzar's idea of human history, the great accomplishment of humanity and humanism. Now we'll see God's viewpoint of the nations and their moral character.

Daniel conveys prophetic truth through signs and symbols, just as John did in the book of Revelation.

FOUR SEA MONSTERS

In the first year of Belshazzar king of Babylon, Daniel had a dream, and visions passed through his mind as he was lying on his bed. He wrote down the substance of his dream.

Daniel said: "In my vision at night I looked, and there before me were the four winds of heaven churning up the great sea. Four great beasts, each different from the others, came up out of the sea." (Dan. 7:1–3)

These beasts were not the predecessors of the Loch Ness monster, but creatures who were symbolic of the nature of certain kingdoms. They emerged out of the great sea, which in ancient times referred to the Mediterranean. In his dream, Daniel saw himself standing by the Mediterranean, but he wasn't there to admire the sunset.

We often use the expression, "a sea of humanity," and the Bible often refers to a "sea" as masses of people. When Daniel in his vision looks at this great sea of humanity, it is being blown from the four corners of the earth, depicting political strife and uprisings, wars and bloodshed among the nations. He sees the nations in unrest, which is the everlasting human condition.

Out of these turbulent waters emerge four of the ugliest zoo animals you can imagine. In the Bible, animals are often used to represent kingdoms, and even today the lion represents Great Britain, the eagle is the United States. Most nations have their own animal symbols.

The first beast who reared its ugly head looked like a lion, but it had the wings of an eagle. As Daniel watched, those wings were torn off and the beast stood up like a man. The second beast looked like a bear and it "had three ribs in its mouth between its teeth. It was told, 'Get up and eat your fill of flesh!'" (Dan. 7:5). The third beast was a four-headed monster that looked like a leopard and had four wings. (Even Dr. Seuss would have had a hard time inventing that.) The fourth beast was almost indescribable. "There before me was a fourth beast—terrifying and frightening and very powerful. It had large iron teeth; it crushed and devoured its victims and trampled underfoot whatever was left. It was different from all the former beasts, and it had ten horns" (Dan. 7:7).

These beasts didn't come up all at once; they followed each other in a sequence. Each represents a chronology of the kingdoms of the world, exactly as it was in Nebuchadnezzar's dream in chapter 2. In the king's viewpoint, they were the physical parts of a human being. (The head of gold: Babylon; the arms and breast of silver: Medo-Persia; the belly of brass: Greece; and the things of iron: Rome.) From God's viewpoint, they were bestial; their true character was revealed.

The first beast was a lion with wings. The national symbol of Babylon was a winged lion. In fact, we have discovered that the Ishtar gates of the city of Babylon show two winged lions guarding the gates. The power and the strength of the Babylonian empire was in the strength and power of the lion and the eagle. Jeremiah described Nebuchadnezzar, "A lion has come out of his lair; a destroyer of nations has set out" (Jer. 4:7).

God gives us specific prophecies, and they are always 100 percent right. Anyone who uses the term *prophet* or *seer* today has to have the same record or be labeled a fraud.

When the winged lion had its wings plucked off, it was just like old King Nebuchadnezzar, when his arrogance and pride caused him to live like a beast for seven years, walking on all fours and eating grass out in the backyard. After a time, he was allowed to stand up like a man again, and he was given a new heart.

The second beast in sequence symbolizes the next kingdom, Medo-Persia. The bears in the Bible are always vicious, not a gentle teddy bear dancing at the end of a rope. The second kingdom was ferocious and greedy, and historians tell us that the Medo-Persians conquered Lydia, Babylon, and Egypt, which are the three ribs Daniel saw in the bear's mouth. The beast was lifted up on one side, like a circus bear doing tricks, and historians tell us that one-half of the Medo-Persian Empire was dominant. The Persians took over and subjugated the Medes, so they became a part of the Persian Empire.

The third beast leaps out of the sea like a leopard springing upon its prey. This animal is known as swift, cunning, cruel, and with an insatiable appetite for blood. History records the fact that the Persians were defeated by Greece, under the leadership of Alexander the Great, who was the progenitor of the military strategy called the blitzkrieg. The lightning character of his conquest is without precedent in the ancient world. This leopard creature had four heads, and as history proves, when Alexander the Great died, his kingdom was divided among his four leading generals.

Alexander and thirty-five thousand soldiers went up against the Medo-Persian army of some two or three hundred thousand men and miraculously won. Everybody said it was the military strategy of Alexander, but in Daniel 7:6, it says this beast was "given authority to rule." No matter how brilliant we may appear, it is ultimately God who is in control.

Poor Alexander could conquer anything but himself, like a lot of world leaders. We are told that he died of dissipation at the age of thirty-two, a drunkard and a victim of his own lusts.

There is no other animal in all the animal kingdom that we can compare to the fourth beast. It represented the imperialistic, cruel materialism of Rome, the empire that was known for its cruelty.

It was Rome that crucified Peter and beheaded Paul. It was Rome that banished John to the island of Patmos, and Rome that burned Christians and butchered men, women, and children. It was Rome that crucified our Lord.

Note how we see the gradual deterioration of the nations. With Nebuchadnezzar we saw the dream begin with the head of gold and end with mud on the feet. In Daniel's first dream, we began with the noble lion, the king of the beasts, and ended with some nondescript creature. This is the devolution of the kingdoms of the world.

THAT WEIRD FOURTH KINGDOM

The Bible says this fourth beast out of the waters had ten horns on his head, which are ten kingdoms who rule simultaneously. Then one will appear who conquers three others and eventually dominates the entire empire. Obviously, we are talking about the Antichrist. There has never been a ten-part Roman Empire in the history of the world, so this has to be future. The Roman Empire never completely disappeared, as did other ancient kingdoms. Rome fell apart because of internal corruption, but the nations of Western Europe and those adjacent to the Mediterranean are still a part of what once was the Roman Empire. When the Germans and the Slavs advanced into the Roman territory, their princes intermarried with Roman families. Charlemagne was descended from a Roman house, almost at the same time that the German emperor, Otto II, and the Russian Grand Prince Vladimir intermarried with daughters of the East Roman emperor. The old Roman kingdom continued, but without dominion.

Remember the ten toes of the beast and the stone cut out of the mountain that came and crushed those toes? This simply means that when Christ comes again the ten-part empire has to be in place.

As Daniel was thinking about those ten horns, a little horn "came up among them; and three of the first horns were uprooted before it" (Dan. 7:8). This horn was unlike any we have ever seen, for it had the eyes of a man and a boastful mouth. You might say he was tooting his own horn. We'll learn more about him later.

WHAT THE HISTORY BOOKS DON'T TELL

From our point of view, we are more "civilized" today. We have bathtubs and gas barbecues, computers and electric cars. We put men on the moon and move our combat troops all around the world. We glory in the advances and achievements of civilization, but God clearly sees human history as a chronicle of immorality, brutality, and depravity. Governments and political leaders may mask their true character from people for a time, but they are unmasked before God. Just as we have moved from the head of gold to the feet of mud, from the royal lion to the nondescript beast, as history unfolds it does not get better, it gets worse.

Human history will not continue indefinitely on its present course, nor will it come to an end with mankind annihilating itself. The world does not seem as paranoid about massive nuclear destruction as it was a short time ago, but there is still the specter of the button being pushed by some demagogue. When Jesus Christ returns, it will be to a world that is still here, not a scorched earth of nuclear waste.

Some people refuse to read the news or watch television because the news is depressing. I like to keep abreast of current events, for when we see nation after nation come and go with coups, plots, and rebellions, the chaos is like the turmoil of the sea that Daniel saw in his dream and is a reminder that what we have never been able to accomplish, God in heaven has in control.

Daniel's dream of the four beasts is not over. In the middle, the scene changes dramatically. It is like sitting in a darkened room, watching his vision on a motion picture screen that is split horizontally into two parts. On the lower half of the screen the four beasts are revealed, coming out of the sea of humanity one after another. As we watch with horror and fascination, the fourth beast appears on the screen, devouring and breaking in pieces all of the nations. With the last gasp of the Roman Empire on earth, suddenly the upper level of the screen lights up and we get a glimpse into the throne room of heaven. What an awesome contrast to the turmoil on earth!

Before we view this majestic scene, we need a prophetic perspective. When we are able to understand the way in which the Old Testament prophets looked at the future, the entire prophetic puzzle will fit together.

MOUNTAINS AND VALLEYS OF PROPHECY

The Old Testament prophet looked ahead and often saw images of the future converge together, without any distinction between the separate advents of Jesus Christ. It's like being a long way from a mountain range. As we drive toward the mountains, it looks like there's one gigantic peak out there. The closer we get, the more we realize that there's not one peak, but two. And as we drive on, we see there's a great valley between those peaks. Daniel, Isaiah, and Jeremiah looked to the future and saw the coming of Jesus Christ as the Messiah, but their prophecies seem to teach us that what happens at the Second Coming happened at the same time as the first coming.

This problem of the great gaps in time of the Old Testament prophecies and their fulfillment in the future has caused a great deal of problems for Bible students. But when we see this time gap with clarity, we will no longer be confused by the sequence described by the prophets of old.

Let's take just one passage in Isaiah 61:

> The Spirit of the Sovereign LORD is on me,
>
> because the LORD has anointed me
>
> to preach good news to the poor.
>
> He has sent me to bind up the brokenhearted,
>
> to proclaim freedom for the captives
>
> and release from darkness for the prisoners,
>
> to proclaim the year of the LORD's favor
>
> and the day of vengeance of our God. (Isa. 61:1–2)

That is a prophecy concerning the coming of Jesus Christ to this earth, and it says that when He returns He is going to preach good news, help the brokenhearted, proclaim liberty for the captives, open the prisons of those who are bound, and proclaim the year of the Lord's favor (not a calendar year, but the period when salvation would be proclaimed—the Messianic age). These terms describe precisely what Jesus did when He first came to earth.

But here is the rest of the story: "To proclaim . . . the day of vengeance of our God." Did that happen when Jesus was here the first time? No, that will happen when He comes the second time with a flaming sword to bring judgment upon the nations. Jesus quoted this passage from Isaiah in Luke 4:18–19. However, the Lord recognized that even in the prophesies of Isaiah, there was a great period of more than nineteen hundred years between His first advent and His second.

In Daniel's bestial dream, that period seems to come to an end with the fourth beast that had ten horns and crushed and devoured its victims. Since there is no evidence that there was a ten-part Roman

Empire, we can conclude that we have reached this time gap, the valley we couldn't see before. This is the last phase, which describes the events that are going to take place when the Lord comes back the second time.

This next part of Daniel's dream is removed from the first part by more than two thousand years. We have jumped to the top part of the screen and are going to visit the throne room of heaven.

THE ANCIENT OF DAYS

As I looked,
thrones were set in place,
and the Ancient of Days took his seat.
His clothing was as white as snow;
the hair of his head was white like wool.
His throne was flaming with fire,
and its wheels were all ablaze.
A river of fire was flowing,
coming out from before him.
Thousands upon thousands attended him;
ten thousand times ten thousand stood before him.
The court was seated,
and the books were opened. (Dan. 7:9–10)

Daniel 7 is the only place in the Bible where the Ancient of Days is mentioned! God is not human; He is a Spirit. But here Daniel is visualizing God as literally "the elderly One," or "the One who has been around forever." As he looks at Him he sees Him in His holiness, eternity, and glory; almost all of the major attributes of God the Father are pictured in the scene that Daniel sees when he looks into heaven.

God is eternal, the Ancient of Days, the source of time. Psalm 90:2 says, "Before the mountains were born or you brought forth the earth and the world, from everlasting to everlasting you are God."

His clothing was white as snow, the picture of absolute purity. As He sits on His throne, it is with majesty, the sovereign judge of the universe, undergirded with fiery wheels which allow Him to bring judgment anywhere in the universe. The "river of fire" depicts God's presence, which is described in many other passages. "Fire goes before him and consumes his foes on every side" (Ps. 97:3).

Billions of angels bow down and worship before the throne of the Ancient of Days, depicting His deity and His Godhead, for He alone is worthy to be worshiped.

Now the court is about to convene, the judge is seated, and the written evidence is produced. God's library of books will be brought out to be reviewed. I don't know all of the books He has in His library, but I know about some of them. Moses knew about one of them when he said, "But now, please forgive their sin—but if not, then blot me out of the book you have written" (Exod. 32:32).

SOME OF GOD'S BOOKS

Did you know that God keeps a record of our sorrows? "Record my lament; list my tears on your scroll—are they not in your record?" (Ps. 56:8). On the library shelf of heaven, God has a book called *The Tears of the Saints*.

There is also a book where God keeps a record of everyone who holds Him in reverence and fears him. "A scroll of remembrance was written in his presence concerning those who feared the LORD and honored his name" (Mal. 3:16). His library also contains the Old and New Testaments, and the book of the acts we have performed, the words we have spoken, and the thoughts we have thought. In fact, in the book of Revelation we see how God will judge the dead as they stand before Him, and the Book of Life is opened.

In Daniel's dream, God is about to open the books and judge the nations of the world. He is going to read their activity, their blasphemy, and their idolatry. He is going to bring Babylon, Medo-Persia, Greece, and Rome before the almighty tribunal and judge them guilty.

If we remember the split-screen image, we can see that the Most High is reigning in heaven, and His enemies are creating turmoil on earth. God is in control.

THE SON OF MAN BEFORE THE THRONE

When Daniel recounted the next player in this heavenly drama, this Person had not yet come to earth as a babe and assumed humanity. "In my vision at night I looked, and there before me was one like a son of man, coming with the clouds of heaven. He approached the Ancient of Days and was led into his presence" (Dan. 7:13).

Students of prophecy know that one of the names of Jesus Christ that is often used in prophetic passages is the Son of Man. The Son of God speaks of His deity; the Son of David speaks of His royalty; and the Son of Man speaks of His humanity.

Now He is in His human form and approaches God the Father. The scene stretches our spiritual imagination to extremes. As Jesus Christ, the Son of Man, stands before the throne, God the Father is going to give Him the nations of the world. In Psalm 2:8 God is speaking, and I believe He is speaking to Jesus Christ. He says, "Ask of me, and I will make the nations your inheritance, the ends of the earth your possession."

Revelation 11:15 puts it this way: "The kingdom of the world has become the kingdom of our Lord and of his Christ, and he will reign for ever and ever."

How did Jesus Christ get the right to rule over all the peoples of every nation? Some people want us to believe that He was just another prophet, a good teacher. He was even given the title *Jesus Christ, Superstar* in a rock musical in the 1970s. To give Him any of those identities is to diminish and degrade who He really is. One day He stood before God the Father and was given complete dominion over the world. His kingdom supersedes everything we have seen in any kingdom, past or future. It is toward His kingdom that we look as Christians to the future. All other governments and world leadership will ultimately fail.

KINGDOM OF CHRIST VS. KINGDOMS OF THE WORLD

We live in the kingdom of this world. It is limited in scope, but the kingdom of Christ is without limitation. He is the absolute monarch of the whole world.

Second, the kingdom of Jesus Christ is unique. It is a kingdom that has about it the aura of the Godhead. It is filled with deity, a glorious kingdom. There have been times in the history of the world that have been considered the golden ages, but we have never seen anything like what God has in store when He sets up His kingdom.

Third, the kingdom is unified while the kingdoms of this world are torn. As we've looked at the book of Daniel, we have seen chaos and disruption in government. This has never stopped. One day I read the newspaper and see that a country has won a war; the next day I find out the war is still going on and no one is victorious. One day there's a truce somewhere, and the next day the truce isn't working.

When Jesus comes to set up His kingdom, it is going to stretch from the east to the west, from the north to the south. It is going to cover every corner of the globe. His kingdom will be unending, while the kingdoms of this world are temporary. Finally, the Scripture tells us it is unconquerable; His kingdom shall not be destroyed.

When we get excited about the kingdom of Jesus Christ, we are going to become sick of the kingdoms of this world. When we see what God has in store for those who love Him, it certainly helps us to understand what is going on in our world today and to not become paranoid about it.

Although he had been given a glimpse of the glorious kingdom of God, Daniel said, "I, Daniel, was troubled in spirit, and the visions that passed through my mind disturbed me" (Dan. 7:15). It's no wonder, for the next frame would disturb any of us. In it we see the ugly, perverse, true meaning of the fourth beast.

12

THE COMING BEAST
AND HIS ANIMAL
KINGDOM

A friend of mine told me about a frantic call he received from a woman who had rented a house from him. She was shrieking so loudly he could barely understand her. "Get over here right away, they're swarming all over the place. It's horrible, just horrible," she wailed.

When he arrived, he found the distraught woman sitting on the kitchen floor, surrounded by the food she was placing in the cabinets. She was near hysteria and kept pointing at the base of the cupboards and crying, "There were millions of them, swarming all over my groceries. When I turned on the light, they disappeared." The exterminator was called immediately to rid the place of the cockroaches.

Satan is like those cockroaches. He does not like to be revealed, and whenever someone turns the light on him, exposing his disguises, he takes cover. But he will also try to attack the people who reveal his tactics and motives. Even a stalwart like Daniel was disturbed by what he saw in his dream of the fourth beast.

> Then I wanted to know the true meaning of the fourth beast, which was different from all the others and most terrifying, with its iron teeth and bronze claws—the beast that crushed and devoured its victims and trampled underfoot whatever was left. I also wanted to know about the ten horns on its head and about the other horn that came up, before which three of them fell— the horn that looked more imposing than the others and that had eyes and a mouth that spoke boastfully. (Dan. 7:19–20)

We have seen the ten horns as the ten-nation confederacy that arises out of the revived Roman Empire; now we focus on the identity of the other horn. This is a person with many names and many disguises, the cleverest con artist the world will ever know. There is a wealth of information about him in the Bible, but the seventh chapter of Daniel sets the stage for our understanding of the prophetic phenomena and his leading role.

WHO IS THE ANTICHRIST?

One of the most popular indoor sports of theologians is to try to identify the Antichrist, spoken of by Daniel and by the apostle John. I have had people take me out to lunch and try to guide me through a study in gematria, which is a method of interpreting the Scripture by equating a person's name with numbers. Since the Antichrist is given the number 666 in Revelation 16:18, there is a formula by which some try to equate the numbers to letters and find out who the person is. Here are the rules you have to follow if you want to make the formula work. First, if the proper name doesn't work, add a title. Second, if it doesn't work in English, try Hebrew, Greek, or Latin. Third, if none of these work, cheat on the spelling. That way you can make anybody the Antichrist.

Before the Protestant Reformation, the most accepted idea was that the Antichrist was the Catholic pope. Saint Bernard in the twelfth century called Pope Anacletus the Antichrist. In the thirteenth century, Frederick II, ruler of the Holy Roman Empire, accused Pope Gregory IX of being the Antichrist. It wasn't the Protestants doing the name calling, it was the Catholics who had fallen out of favor with the papal regime that was in power at that time.

Not only disgruntled Catholics, but also some of the most responsible Protestant scholars and theologians were convinced that the Antichrist was living in Rome disguised as the pope. The list is impressive: Martin Luther, leader of the Protestant Reformation; Philip Melanchthon, German reformer; John Calvin, French reformer in Geneva; Huldreich Zwingli, Swiss reformer; William Tyndale, English reformer and Bible translator. All of these illustrious men and more pointed their fingers at the pope as the guilty one.

People today continue to play the game. From Judas Iscariot to political leaders of our day, the speculations continue.

I don't know who the Antichrist is, but I do know what he is. From the time of Daniel and the Babylonian kingdom to the end of human government when Christ the King returns, God gives us the whole scheme of things to come and descriptions of this infamous individual.

HIS NAMES ARE LEGION

As we read through the Scripture, we find many names for the Antichrist and unless we know them, it is easy to get confused. In the seventh chapter of Daniel he is called "the little horn," which is a phrase used to describe power and authority. The eighth chapter calls him "a fierce-looking king" (v. 23), and in chapter 9 he is "the ruler who will come" (v. 26). Later, Daniel says he is the willful king (11:36).

In the New Testament he is called "the man of lawlessness" (2 Thess. 2:3), "the antichrist" (1 John 2:18), and "a beast coming out of the sea" (Rev. 13:1). Many names and many disguises are attributed to Satan's progeny.

We now begin to see his character by some descriptions in Daniel's dream. He is a charismatic leader. I'm not talking about his doctrine, but his compelling manner. In several places in the seventh chapter we read in the King James Version that he has "a mouth speaking great things" (v. 8), "a mouth that spake very great things" (v. 20), and, "he shall speak great words against the most High" (v. 25).

In the thirteenth chapter of Revelation, which is the comparative study to the seventh chapter of Daniel, it says, "And there was given unto him a mouth speaking great things" (v. 5 kjv). In fact, a little later on in the program of the Antichrist, he establishes a great image that everybody is supposed to worship, and even this image speaks. Some people think he does it through ventriloquism, some think it is demon possession, but whatever it is, this man has great oratorical power.

He will not only be a tremendous speaker, but he will be extremely attractive. The little horn "looked more imposing than the others" (Dan. 7:20). When this man walks into a room, he will capture everyone's attention. He will have an inhuman magnetism that will draw people to him.

Politicians do not command great respect today, but the Antichrist will be the master politician of all history, the greatest diplomat who ever lived. Verse 20 says he "had eyes," and that phrase refers to his mental intellect and cleverness. He will be able to solve the problems of the world with superhuman wisdom.

It says that the "other horn . . . came up, before which three of them fell" (Dan. 7:20). What this means is that the Antichrist moves in and replaces three of the nations by some sort of political subterfuge and somehow maneuvers them until he arrogates their power to himself. His cleverness is described in Daniel 11:21, where it says "he will seize it through intrigue." The King James Version calls it "flatteries." You can combine all the malarkey you have ever heard during political campaigns, all the candidates' promises and solemn vows, and the Antichrist will be master of them all. He'll be able to talk people into anything.

He is also a cultic leader, a person who considers himself a religious man. "He will speak against the Most High and oppress his saints and try to change the set times and the laws" (Dan. 7:25). He wants to take over for God and is going to ask people to fall down and worship him. Revelation 13:8 says, "All inhabitants of the earth will worship the beast." He will even try to change the moral and natural laws of the universe. Some think he even does away with the seven-day week, which is a God-ordered time period. He even tries to change the calendar and do away with all the religious feast days. He tries to strip down everything that has anything to do with order and structure and rewrite the way the world should function. He will eliminate all moral laws so that our society, which has some degree of values, will become completely lawless.

How will a man like that ever get enough people to follow him so he can rule the world? The Scripture says he will be equipped by Satan to do great miracles, signs, and wonders. I believe he will bring people back from the grave and heal people in a manner that the world has not seen since Jesus walked upon this earth. If we look at the way people flock to healing services today, it will not be difficult to understand how the Antichrist will get his followers.

When we think of the cruelest man in recent history, both Hitler and Stalin come to mind. But the Scripture says that in the end of time the Antichrist "will devour the whole earth, trampling it down and crushing it" (Dan. 7:23). And he "shall wear out the saints of the most High" (Dan. 7:25 KJV).

The people who are saved during the Tribulation period become the target of this man, and he determines to destroy them. We need to understand that people who have never heard the gospel of Jesus Christ may be living during the Tribulation period, and many of them will become believers. However, their lives will be in treacherous situations; many of them will be martyred for their faith. It may be a slow, torturous wearing down of the people of God. He may wear them out through public seizure, certainly through economic squeeze. He will undoubtedly starve some of them to death.

INTO THE VACUUM OF LEADERSHIP

There are some things going on in the world today that make the study of the Antichrist very important to us. The world is ripe for a leader who will come upon the scene and command the respect and following of the people. One lesson from history shows us how economic conditions helped catapult a demagogue into power.

The German treasury after World War I was low in gold, the budget was unbalanced, and inflation went out of sight. In 1919, the German mark was worth twenty-five cents. Within four years it declined in value until four trillion marks were needed to equal the buying power of one dollar. The German middle class lost all its savings and every pension was wiped out. The people were ready to listen to anyone who would help them solve their bitterness. In

Russia, it was Lenin who said, "The surest way to overthrow an existing social order is to debauch the currency."

What do you think would happen if a miracle-working, brilliant leader were to walk across the American scene and say, "I have the answer to all the economic stress of this country?" Do you think anyone would follow him?

In spite of the fact that this person has yet to appear, he may be living today, polishing his skills until his time comes. The Bible says his spirit is already here. "Every spirit that does not acknowledge Jesus is not from God. This is the spirit of the antichrist, which you have heard is coming and even now is already in the world" (1 John 4:3). Another warning says, "Dear children, this is the last hour; and as you have heard that the antichrist is coming, even now many antichrists have come" (1 John 2:18).

All the cultists and New Agers indicate to us that what John said was true. The spirit of Antichrist is everywhere in the world today, and false messiahs are on every horizon.

Although there are only a few references to the Antichrist in Daniel, his prophecies are the forerunners of Revelation, and Revelation interprets Daniel. The two of them taken together outline the scheme of events for the future, which gives any Bible Christian a map to chart the course of events in our day. The thirteenth chapter of Revelation describes the battle strategy of the Antichrist.

REIGN OF TERROR

In Revelation 13 the Scripture says that the Antichrist is truly Satan's masterpiece. He is the essence of Satan's desire wrapped up in one person, all that Satan ever longed for in his ministry. No wonder he is such a frightening personality.

Just as God gave Daniel his prophetic dreams, He also gave

John the vision of things to come. Separated by almost six centuries, the two men are given the same prophecies.

John said, "And I saw a beast coming out of the sea. He had ten horns and seven heads, with ten crowns on his horns, and on each head a blasphemous name" (Rev. 13:1). We know that "sea" refers to masses of people. The Antichrist will begin his ministry behind the scenes before he is finally brought out to center stage. The times will be tumultuous. There will be political turmoil and a lack of leadership.

John sees him with seven heads, and later in his book tells us, "The seven heads are seven hills on which the woman sits" (Rev. 17:9). The "woman" is the harlot, the representative of the false religious system of the end times. The seven heads being the seven mountains clearly identifies Rome, or the corresponding kingdoms out of the Holy Roman Empire.

John also tells us, "The beast I saw resembled a leopard, but had feet like those of a bear and a mouth like that of a lion" (Rev. 13:2). Remember the consecutive kingdoms that Daniel described? Babylon was the lion, Medo-Persia the bear, and Greece the leopard. In other words, this beast combines the strength, brutality, and swiftness of these kingdoms. He will be a Nebuchadnezzar-Cyrus-Caesar-Alexander, with some Hitler-Mao-Stalin bound together in one personality.

"One of the heads of the beast seemed to have had a fatal wound, but the fatal wound had been healed. The whole world was astonished and followed the beast" (Rev. 13:3). Satan is playing his old counterfeit game again. Just as Jesus Christ came to the cross and died, was buried and resurrected, so Satan does the same thing with his offspring. Just as the resurrection of Christ caused the church to grow with a tremendous spiritual renewal, the resurrection of the Antichrist will cause the world to follow him.

Now everyone will worship the Antichrist. Those whose names have been written in the Lamb's Book of Life will be the notable exception. They will refuse his mark and defy his orders. What incredible feats of bravery will be performed during the Tribulation. We have no concept of the horrors the Tribulation believers will endure.

The masses will follow the Antichrist, not only because of his charismatic personality and miraculous revival from a fatal head wound, but also because of his great military exploits. Once he has brought together three nations out of the European confederacy and has control over them, he will overpower the remaining European nations. Then the Scripture says he does a very wise thing. He realizes the Jews are a problem and that he needs to deal with them. So he will go to Israel and make a covenant with the Jewish people. He says he will allow them to continue their worship and temple practices, but after three and a half years he will break his promise (of course) and walk into the temple and desecrate it and begin a threefold program that he believes will give him absolute control in the world.

His control will be religious, political, and economic. He will have everyone under his command, except those written in the Book of Life.

We are called to attention by the apostle John when he writes, "He who has an ear, let him hear." Sit up and take notice! "If anyone is to be killed with the sword, with the sword he will be killed. This calls for patient endurance and faithfulness on the part of the saints" (Rev. 13:10).

Although the reign of the Antichrist is worldwide and his dominion without peer, the end is in sight! The Bible says that the Antichrist and his followers will come to war with Jesus Christ and His followers, and Christ will be the victor.

Then I saw the beast and the kings of the earth and their armies gathered together to make war against the rider on the horse and his army. But the beast was captured, and with him the false prophet who had performed the miraculous signs on his behalf. With these signs he had deluded those who had received the mark of the beast and worshiped his image. The two of them were thrown alive into the fiery lake of burning sulfur. (Rev. 19:19–20)

I get excited when I study this, because I am on the winning side. I know all about the fight, but I'm confident about the winner. I've cast my lot with the King of kings.

OUR STRATEGY

The strategy for the Christian is not to look for the Antichrist, but to at least know what his plans are. I'm not looking around and guessing who and where the Antichrist is. He might be alive today, and he might be strutting on the stage of politics at this time, but speculation about him does not fit either of the two things God has told us to do in the light of the coming Christ. Those two simple things are first to work: "Occupy till I come" (Luke 19:13 KJV). There was a time, particularly in the 1970s, that many people thought it was useless to work hard, buy life insurance, or make any plans for the future, because they thought Christ was going to return soon. This is not what He told us. He said to work until He comes.

The second thing is this: "Therefore keep watch, because you do not know the day or the hour" (Matt. 25:13). So our job, in light of the fact that we are looking for Christ, is to work and to watch. When I see all these things happening that tell me the Antichrist is coming, it just helps me focus my attention on the coming of Christ.

PART 3

ISRAEL'S FUTURE

13

SUPERPOWERS
IN CONFLICT

When Daniel walked into the hall where Belshazzar and his cronies were having that infamous and fatal party, he knew why doom was at the door. The handwriting on the wall said that the kingdom would be divided and given to the Medes and the Persians. How was he so sure?

In the eighth chapter of Daniel, God is going to communicate to him the information he needs to know when he walks on the scene at the Babylonian going-out party. This vision occurred during the third year of Belshazzar's reign, when Daniel was in his early sixties. God sent His own personal envoy, the angel Gabriel, to relate to His servant Daniel the broad sweep of Gentile history concerning the people of Israel.

The first part of Daniel's epic gives us the view of Gentile history apart from Israel, but now we are coming to that time when Israel and its people are the focal point. God chose to devote a special chapter in His Book to the details about the Medes, Persians, and Greeks because these nations were vital to the history of Israel and the life of the Jews.

The language itself even changes in chapter 8. A shift occurs from Aramaic to Hebrew. Now God is going to uniquely show how He will deal with His people. The land of Israel has been the nerve center of the world since the time of Abraham. When Jesus Christ came to earth, Israel became the truth center of the world. There is coming a day in the future (the Millennium) when that land will be the peace center of the world. Today, as we look at that small piece of real estate in the Middle East, it is the storm center of the world.

HOLY WONDER

How could a man like Daniel be surprised at anything? It's interesting to note his response to God's communication: "In the third year of the reign of king Belshazzar a vision appeared unto me, *even unto me Daniel*" (8:1 KJV, emphasis added). Again he said, "And it came to pass, when I, *even I Daniel*, had seen the vision, and sought for the meaning" (8:15 KJV, emphasis added). When the vision was over and Daniel began to understand what was involved, he was emotionally worn out. "I, Daniel, was exhausted and lay ill for several days" (Dan. 8:27).

If we read the Bible with an apathetic attitude, racing through each book so we can say we've read it from cover to cover, we probably won't understand Daniel's involvement. But just imagine how it would feel to have God speak to you in a vision and tell you what was going to happen to the United States in the years to come. I don't believe God uses visions today to present the future, but if He did, I'm sure I would get sick too.

In his vision, Daniel was transported to Susa, a small, nondescript city in Babylon. He saw himself standing by a canal in front of the palace. What possible difference could it make that God's man in Babylon was somewhere out in the suburbs, on the bank of an unremarkable waterway? This town wouldn't even rate a large red dot on the map. But this place was going to be the very nerve center of the next kingdom. Babylon was a falling star, and the Persian Empire was about to begin.

In the Old Testament, the Persian literature of Nehemiah and Esther talk of Susa. Nehemiah said, "In the month of Kislev in the twentieth year, while I was in the citadel of Susa" (Neh. 1:1). And in Esther, King Xerxes reigned from his royal throne in the citadel of Susa (Esth. 1:2). We see another important link in prophecy when we understand that long before the Persian Empire began, before Babylon fell, Daniel saw himself at the capital of the Persian kingdom. God doesn't leave loose ends in His prophecy parade.

THE RAM

While Daniel was standing beside the canal, he said,

> I looked up, and there before me was a ram with two horns, standing beside the canal, and the horns were long. One of the horns was longer than the other but grew up later. I watched the ram as he charged toward the west and the north and the south. No animal could stand against him, and none could rescue from his power. He did as he pleased and became great. (Dan. 8:3–4)

We don't need to go to an encyclopedia to find out who this ram is, because in verse 20 we are told that the two-horned ram represents the kings of Media and Persia. After the Babylonian kingdom fell, the Medes stepped in first and were joined by the Persians. Soon we don't hear any more about the Medes, for the Persians assimilated the whole Median kingdom, just as prophecy says.

Cyrus the Persian and his son, Cambesis II, built the largest empire the world had ever seen to that day. It moved in every direction, and no other kingdom could stand before them.

ENTER THE GOAT

Daniel continued:

> As I was thinking about this, suddenly a goat with a prominent horn between his eyes came from the west, crossing the whole earth without touching the ground. He came toward the two-horned ram I had seen standing beside the canal and charged at him in great rage. I saw him attack the ram furiously, striking the ram and shattering his two horns. The ram was powerless to stand against him; the goat knocked him to the ground and trampled on him, and none could rescue the ram from his power. (Dan. 8:5–7)

This is one of the most amazing passages I've ever read in the prophetic word. First, the identification of the goat is not difficult. The Grecian Empire followed that of the Medo-Persians. The first Greek colony was established by an oracle that sent a goat for a guide to build a city. The goat came to the region of Greece, and in gratitude for the goat's leading them in the right direction, they called the city Agae, meaning "The Goat City." The name of the sea upon whose shores the city was built was called the Aegean Sea, or the "Goat Sea."

Five amazing prophecies are made in this passage that were fulfilled in history down to the minutest detail. First, as we've just discussed, the goat represents Greece, and the later explanation for the large horn between his eyes is that of the first king. As the goat began to expand its holdings and cover the whole earth, it moved so rapidly that its feet didn't seem to touch the ground. It set world records for bringing the known world under its dominion. History tells us that Greece built a kingdom like no other kingdom before it. In twelve brief years, the Greeks conquered the entire civilized world without losing a battle. Greece became the dominant force in the world faster than any other kingdom before it, and God had said that was how it was going to happen some two hundred years earlier.

The second amazing prophecy has to do with the reputation of the king. He is called "a prominent horn" or a "notable horn." What a name for a man like Alexander the Great. When he was growing up, his mother taught him that he was the descendant of Achilles and Hercules. No wonder the kid was motivated. When he was just a little boy there was a horse that everyone in his family had tried to break, but no one could do it. Alexander said, "I'll do it!" And he did. According to historians, that was the horse that he rode in all of the great campaigns as he led the Greeks in their conquest of the world.

His father, Philip of Macedon, was a great military man, and we are told that Alexander used to spend most of his time worrying that there wouldn't be anything left for him to conquer because his father was such a great military leader. After a particularly significant victory by Philip, he pulled his son aside and said, "Alexander, my son, seek out a kingdom worthy of yourself. Macedonia is too small for you." What an encouraging dad. He was saying, "Son, you're greater than I am. Go for something big!" And Alexander thought, *I'll go for the world.*

I wonder how much of his success was built into him because of the faith his parents had in him. Kids need to know we believe that they can do great things, better than we ever did or hoped to do. Philip of Macedon certainly wasn't a Christian, but he knew how to inspire his son.

The third prophecy has to do with the ruin of the Medo-Persian Empire. God said to Daniel that when the notable horn, the great king, comes to power, he is going to come against the Persians and the Medes. "I saw him attack the ram furiously, striking the ram and shattering his two horns. The ram was powerless to stand against him; the goat knocked him to the ground and trampled on him, and none could rescue the ram from his power" (Dan. 8:7).

When Alexander decided to take down the Medes and the Persians, he came with thirty-five thousand troops from the west, crossed over the Hellespont, and defeated the Persian army. He swept on south and took Egypt, Tyre, and Gaza, and then he retraced his steps through Syria and met an enlarged Persian army for the third time. Then he did just what the Scripture said. He threw them to the ground, stomped on them, and the Medo-Persian Empire was wiped out, just as predicted.

The fourth remarkable prophecy in this passage has to do with the death of the king. The Scripture says, "The goat became very great, but at the height of his power his large horn was broken off, and in its place four prominent horns grew up toward the four winds of heaven" (Dan. 8:8).

After Alexander had conquered the Medo-Persians, he swept on to India, but his tired army had had enough and returned to Babylon. Alexander died there at the age of thirty-three, a victim of his own drunkenness and depression because there weren't any more worlds to conquer.

Two hundred years before Alexander died, God described in the minutest detail exactly how history was going to be written. A story was told that when Alexander was on his way to Jerusalem to conquer that city, one of the Jewish priests gave him a copy of the book of Daniel and said, "You've got to read this. You're in here!" Alexander read the prophecy, and it was said that he got down on his knees and worshiped. However, he did not save himself from an early death, just as it was foretold.

As Alexander was sweeping over the civilized earth, he thought he was doing his own work. He believed all of his achievements were products of his own genius, but he was just filling out the outline of prophecy that God had given. Great as he was, he was nothing more than a tool, an instrument of God. Although he didn't realize it, Alexander accomplished certain feats that God had sent him to do. These achievements needed doing before Jesus Christ could come.

When Alexander amassed all these kingdoms, he was concerned about the many different languages and cultures. He decided that he would Hellenize the world, which means he would bring it all under Greek culture. Consequently, he established the Greek language we know today as Koine Greek. He taught all of the people he had conquered this language and the culture of Greece, so they would understand how they were supposed to live. He probably didn't know he was preparing the way for the Scriptures to be written in Greek. (This is the reason many seminaries teach Greek, so those of us in the ministry can more accurately interpret the meaning in the Scriptures.)

Then he became concerned about the ability to have access to his great kingdom, so he built vast highways and roads to all the provinces over which he had control. When he moved off the scene at the age of thirty-three, the roads had been prepared upon which the missionaries would travel and the language had been established in which the gospel could be written and preached.

Alexander never knew how he was being used to prepare the world for the coming of Jesus Christ and the dissemination of the gospel. He thought he was doing his own thing!

The last part of this prophecy has to do with four horns that replaced the great horn but would not have the same power. When Alexander died, his kingdom was divided, and history tells us that four of his generals literally fulfilled that prophecy. These four formed separate kingdoms out of the empire Alexander had created. From one of those kingdoms came a ruler who surpassed all the others in cruelty and hatred for the Jews and their religion.

Daniel was given a historical preview of this man of evil, but the prophecy had a dual fulfillment. One part was fulfilled in a man who was born 175 years before Christ, and the second part will be fulfilled in the future. Over and over again we see that we can trust the Bible for our future, since it is completely reliable in its predictions of the past.

FORESHADOWS OF THE FINAL GENTILE RULER

Alexander the Great had some qualities we could admire. As we look with Daniel at the sad failure of Alexander at the climax of his career, it should make us wonder about the conquerors in history. Alexander's fall was due to the overexhausting commitment he made to his cause. The brilliance of his success brought about his early death. It's often true that with the fortunes of individuals and societies, the battle is won, but the war is lost.

After the infighting was over and Alexander's kingdom was divided, out of the Seleucid kingdom came a man who started insignificantly but became the most diabolical ruler of his day.

> Out of one of them came another horn, which started small but grew in power to the south and to the east and toward the Beautiful Land. It grew until it reached the host of the heavens, and it threw some of the starry host down to the earth and

trampled on them. It set itself up to be as great as the Prince of the host; it took away the daily sacrifice from him, and the place of his sanctuary was brought low. Because of rebellion, the host of the saints and the daily sacrifice were given over to it. It prospered in everything it did, and truth was thrown to the ground. (Dan. 8:9–12)

You may never have heard of this man in your ancient history courses in school, but this prophecy was fulfilled in a person named Antiochus Epiphanes. His name means "Antiochus, God Manifest." Diabolical arrogance was his nature. After trying to conquer the world and being stopped by Roman armies, he turned his fury on Jerusalem and sacked the city. He killed some eighty thousand Jews and sold another forty thousand into slavery.

To kill the Jews was one thing, but to destroy their faith was another. Antiochus decided to substitute Greek worship and culture for the Jewish religion. Instead of the Jewish Feast of the Tabernacles, he brought into the temple the Feast of Bacchanalia, worshiping Bacchus, the god of pleasure and wine. He forbade the observance of the Sabbath and the reading of the Scripture, even burning every copy of the Torah he could find. The Jews in the city were forbidden to practice anything Jewish on penalty of death.

One Greek general under the direction of Antiochus set up some games outside the temple. That doesn't sound so bad, but all of the people who participated in the games were stripped naked, including the Jewish priests and everyone who was a part of Jewish worship. It was extreme humiliation.

The Jews were forbidden the practice of circumcision, and history records there were two mothers who, because of their deep commitment to their culture, were determined to circumcise their baby boys. When Antiochus heard about it, he took the babies and killed them, hung them around each mother's neck and marched the women through the streets of Jerusalem to the highest wall. There the women and their babies were thrown headlong over the precipice. Another story was told of a mother who had seven sons who defied Antiochus' law. He cut out the boys' tongues in front of their mother and fried them to death on a flat iron one at a time. Then the mother was murdered. Is it any wonder that the Jews hated this Greek ruler and changed his name to Antiochus Epimanes, which means "Antiochus, the Madman."

When the Bible talks about the desecration of the temple, it is a reference to the moment when Antiochus walked into the sacred place of the Jews with a pig and slit its throat as a sacrifice on the altar of the Jewish people. Then he took the blood from that animal and sprayed it all over the inside of the temple. The Bible speaks of that as the Abomination of Desolation. There was nothing more horrible to the Jews than to have their sacred place profaned by the blood of an unclean animal.

I believe Daniel visualized all of this in his mind more vividly than I could tell you. He saw what was going to happen to his people at a future time as Antiochus the Madman came to rule over and profane his people.

Such consummate evil is not pleasant to read about, but imagine what it would be like to have it unfold in a vision, as Daniel did. As he was seeing this horror, he heard a voice. "Then I heard a holy one speaking, and another holy one said to him, 'How long will it take for the vision to be fulfilled—the vision concerning the daily sacrifice, the rebellion that causes desolation, and the surrender of the sanctuary and of the host that will be trampled underfoot?'" (Dan. 8:13).

If you were a Jewish patriarch and you saw a vision concerning the desolation we've just described, wouldn't you ask, "How long can God let this go on?" The answer was given and fulfilled historically, for it was approximately twenty-three hundred days from the time that the Jewish religion came under persecution by Antiochus to the time of his death. God told Daniel through his vision that the days were numbered.

God used a man to destroy Antiochus. This story is not found in the Bible, but is a favorite of mine, for it explains a special celebration of the Jews that exists to this day.

JUDAS THE HAMMER

In those days of terrible persecution, there was a priest, Mattathias, who lived in a town outside of Jerusalem. He was a great patriarch and grieved over the sorrow of his people. One day an emissary from Antiochus came to the place where Mattathias lived and said, "You are ordered to bow down before the altar of Jupiter, our Greek god." Mattathias was so incensed over this order that when a Jew came to worship Jupiter, the old priest killed the Jew then killed the officer who made the Jew bow. This was the beginning of the Maccabean revolt.

The old priest died, but he passed the torch of liberty and revolution to Judas Maccabeus, his son, who was known as Judas the Hammer. He won the victory over Antiochus and independence for his people. When Judas went back to cleanse the temple in 144 BC, the first thing he wanted to do was find oil to light the lamps. According to tradition, the ceremony that would reconsecrate the temple would take eight days, but when he found only one cruse of oil, he knew he didn't have enough to last for all that time. However, as the story goes, that small amount of oil lasted for the entire eight days. To this day the Jewish people celebrate the feast of reconstruction and dedication of their temple. They call it the feast of Hanukkah, celebrated during our Christmas season. On the first day of Hanukkah, devout Jews light a candle, the second day they light another, and so on until after eight days there are eight candles burning. It is a sign of victory and deliverance, which goes right back to this period in history in the book of Daniel.

I heard a story about a persecutor of the Jews in a country that was at one time behind the Iron Curtain. He asked one of the Jews who had been tortured, "What do you think will happen to you and your people if we continue to persecute you?"

"Ah, the result will be a feast," replied the Jew. "Pharaoh tried to destroy us, and the result was Passover. Haman attempted to destroy us, and the result was the Feast of Purim. Antiochus Epiphanes tried to destroy us, and the result was the Feast of Dedication. Just try to destroy us, and we'll start another feast."

God has demonstrated throughout history the special place the Jewish people have in His heart.

We have looked at vast segments of history, from the leadership of Alexander, who demonstrates for us the power of the coming Antichrist, and the vile Antiochus, who epitomizes the cruelty of the coming Antichrist. He is the one toward whom all of this prophetic information is pointing. When you take Alexander's power, add the cruelty of Antiochus, and magnify that a hundred times, we haven't begun to approach what the Antichrist is going to be like when he comes.

THE MASTER OF INTRIGUE

As certainly as the prophecies of Alexander and Antiochus Epiphanes came true, so the prophecy concerning a "completely wicked, a stern-faced king, a master of intrigue" will come to pass.

It is interesting that the characters of these other two men merge together in what we learn about the Antichrist.

> In the latter part of their reign, when rebels have become completely wicked, a stern-faced king, a master of intrigue, will arise. He will become very strong, but not by his own power. He will cause astounding devastation and will succeed in whatever he does. He will destroy the mighty men and the holy people. He will cause deceit to prosper, and he will consider himself superior. When they feel secure, he will destroy many and take his stand against the Prince of princes. Yet he will be destroyed, but not by human power. (Dan. 8:23–25)

This will be a man who is very dramatic in appearance. People seem to be attracted to someone who is striking, who makes heads turn. He will not be the type who could disappear in a crowd.

Notice when he will arrive. It is when corruption is at an all-time high, when all restraints are lifted, and everything seems to be speeding in the direction of evil. Society will have disintegrated to the point where nothing is sacred; there will be no holds barred. Then he will walk into our world and have all the right answers. I have said that if there would be a man in our world today who could stand up with solutions to our economic problems, the world would do anything to gain prosperity.

This dynamic leader, with the mental ability to solve the problems of his day, will undoubtedly be involved with the occult, for the Scripture says he "will cause deceit to prosper."

His destructiveness will be so universal that the world will reel under his power. Antiochus did the same, but his cruelty was child's play compared to the Antichrist. Everything I know about Antiochus Epiphanes causes me to shudder, but when I think about what the Antichrist is going to be, I can't imagine the magnitude of his depravity.

This man of lawlessness is described in 2 Thessalonians 2:4: "He will oppose and will exalt himself over everything that is called God or is worshiped, so that he sets himself up in God's temple, proclaiming himself to be God."

Old Antiochus had coins printed during his reign that contained four words: *Theos Antiochus Theos Epiphanes*. That means "Antiochus the Great, God Manifest." He said he was god, just like the Antichrist will do when he comes.

The Antichrist will disguise his cruelty with peace promises. When people are feeling secure, he will unleash his powerful destruction. In the next chapter we'll see how that double-cross will take place.

But he will come to a blazing end, not in an electric chair or gas chamber or any other human means. Even in this, Antiochus seems to be a forerunner of the Antichrist. He made great strides in his godless purge, until finally the Jews revolted. They cast the image of Jupiter out of the temple, where he had placed it, which made him so angry that he claimed Jerusalem would become a common burial place for all the Jews. As soon as he made this declaration, he was afflicted with an incurable disease. His suffering was unbearable and the stench from his own body so horrible that he couldn't stand himself. He died in misery, a foolish man who thought he could resist God and get by with it. He was brought down supernaturally without one human hand touching him.

How does this apply to the Antichrist? How does he end? One day King Jesus is going to ride out of glory and go into combat with that wicked man who will be cast into hell, not by human power, but supernaturally.

DANIEL'S REACTION AND OUR RESPONSE

Our friend Daniel had this astounding visitation by the angel Gabriel and it literally made him ill. He was told to "seal up the vision," which means he should preserve it so that it could be communicated later. He followed this command and has given it to all generations of Bible-believing Christians. However, when he saw his people under the persecution of these tyrants and realized that many of them would be killed, it grieved him immensely. He fainted, he got sick, and he became emotional.

If we really appreciate the fact that Daniel was a man who got one little slice of God's plan for the future and it wiped him out, how do we respond? God has given us the entire plan for the world, and many of us sit in our comfort zones with the Bible blahs. I believe God wants us to get serious about this Book. When we read about the coming man of sin, the one who is going to rule this world and destroy those who have been left behind, it should compel us to look at those around us and tell them about the accurate prophecies in God's Word. The prophetic Word of God ought to motivate us to see our planet as a world that is lost. That lost world is falling into the lap of Satan, person by person, because Christian people don't care. If we really believed what Daniel has to tell us, it would change our lives.

14

DOWN ON OUR KNEES

For the third day in a row the morning paper carried a story about the senseless shooting of a child. At the checkout counter in the market the tabloids screamed about another celebrity sexual tryst. Sick news never stops. No wonder depression creates a gray cloud over our heads. But then, why pray when we can worry?

During the reign of Darius the Mede in Babylon, Daniel was premier of the country. He was in his eighties, a man whose long life and position of influence should have allowed him to live a worry-free life. He could have collected his Social Security, wrapped himself in a Persian shawl, and spent his last days in a rocking chair. Instead, he was poring over the books, those scrolls that the exiles had been careful to bring with them from Israel. As he studied the book of Jeremiah, he knew that the exile was almost at an end. Prophecy drove him to his knees, seeking through prayer a closer relationship with his God.

With the books open before him, he could know the same intimacy with God that he experienced many decades before in the temple.

The ninth chapter of Daniel is one of the most important chapters in the Bible. Spiritually, it has one of the greatest Old Testament prayers; prophetically, it contains the most comprehensive outline of the end times.

The prayer is an example of what praying ought to be. It is a masterpiece for us to admire, a dramatic example of principles to follow.

DANIEL'S MOTIVATION, OUR IMITATION

When Daniel went into captivity with the rest of the Jews, he didn't have a copy of the Bible like we have today. He had some portions of the Old Testament, some of which were the writings of Jeremiah. This man was around in the time just before the captivity of the people of Judah. He was the last prophet to call out to the Jews to repent before the judgment of God fell upon them. I believe that when Daniel was in his eighty-fifth or eighty-sixth year, he was having his personal devotions in the book of Jeremiah, and something jumped off the page that motivated him to pray this great prayer.

> In the first year of his [Darius'] reign, I, Daniel, understood from the Scriptures, according to the word of the LORD given to Jeremiah the prophet, that the desolation of Jerusalem would last seventy years. So I turned to the Lord God and pleaded with him in prayer and petition, in fasting, and in sackcloth and ashes. (Dan. 9:2–3)

We weren't there to look over Daniel's shoulder, but I know that these must have been some of the words he was reading:

> Therefore the LORD Almighty says this: "Because you have not listened to my words, I will summon all the peoples of the north

and my servant Nebuchadnezzar king of Babylon," declares the LORD, "and I will bring them against this land and its inhabitants and against all the surrounding nations, I will completely destroy them and make them an object of horror and scorn, and an everlasting ruin. I will banish from them the sounds of joy and gladness, the voices of bride and bridegroom, the sound of millstones and the light of the lamp. This whole country will become a desolate wasteland, and these nations will serve the king of Babylon seventy years." (Jer. 25:8–11)

Daniel had lived through almost seventy years of the captivity. His heart had ached as he watched the song taken out of the hearts of his people as they hung their harps on the willows and cried for the day they might return to Jerusalem. He saw the captivity take the life out of their Jewish culture and history. But that wasn't the part of the prophecy that caught his attention. His eyes, still sharp in spite of his years, must have searched the words on the scrolls until he came to this passage:

This is what the LORD says: "When seventy years are completed for Babylon, I will come to you and fulfill my gracious promise to bring you back to this place. For I know the plans I have for you," declares the LORD, "plans to prosper you and not to harm you, plans to give you hope and a future." (Jer. 29:10–11)

As he read that prophecy, it must have grabbed his heart, because he realized that the time for the return of his people to Jerusalem was drawing near. He probably wasn't sure whether the seventy years was calculated from the first deportation or the second or the third. Daniel and his friends were taken in the first phase, so as he was praying, he was trying to think when those seventy years would be accomplished. But one thing he knew. It was getting close! It was almost time for God to take the Jews back into their land. When Daniel read that prophecy, it affected him so emotionally that he fell to his knees and began to pray.

Isn't it true that when we really come to grips with prophecy, it ought to have that kind of effect on us? Often, however, we get into prophetic studies and want to run around to conferences and read books to compare views with each other. We get so caught up in the exercise of understanding prophetic truth that we miss the whole point. It ought to drive us to our knees, even as it did Daniel. Here was a man who was so intensely involved with God's truth, that when he read what God had to say, he couldn't stay the same. His prayer was motivated by the Word of God.

I have had young people come to me and say, "Pastor Jeremiah, when I have my quiet time, what should I do first? Should I pray first and then read the Bible, or should I read the Bible first and then pray?" I think it is always proper, before we open the Scripture, to briefly ask for God's blessing and insight into the text. But if I understand the priority of the Scriptures, prayer grows out of the Word of God.

A STRANGE, POWERFUL PRINCIPLE OF PRAYER

When Daniel read in the book of Jeremiah that God was going to keep His people in captivity for seventy years and then release them, he believed it. Then a very strange thing happened. He began to pray that God would do what He was going to do. Wait a minute, if God's going to do it, why should we pray? At this point we discover one of the most tremendous principles about prayer.

God knows His plan, and even when He reveals His plan to us, He expects us to pray over that plan. The Bible says, "If we ask anything according to his will, he hears us. And if we know that he hears us—whatever we ask—we know that we have what we asked of him" (1 John 5:14–15).

Sometimes I get the impression that I have misunderstood the meaning of prayer. Prayer is not to get God to change His will. If we really believe the will of God is perfect, then why would we want Him to change it? Our prayers really ought to be prompted out of our deep understanding of what the will of God is. There are a lot of folks who go to prayer, not to ascertain the will of God, but to ask Him to do what they want. Prayer is not getting God to adjust His program to what we want, it is adjusting our lives to the revealed will of God. When we pray, it isn't God who changes, it's us. Maybe we've been looking for change at the wrong end of the cycle.

Daniel understood God's will, and he began to pray that his people would come into conformity with the revealed will of God, so that God could do what He had already said He was going to do. The biggest waste of time in Christendom is praying about things that God already said we shouldn't do. During my years in the ministry many young people have come to me about getting married. For instance, a young girl who is a sweet Christian comes to me when she is ready to get married and wants me to perform the ceremony. She's madly in love with someone who doesn't know the Lord. We sit down and I open the Bible and talk to her about being unequally yoked together, and that God said this was against His will. "Oh, Pastor, I've prayed about this, and I have real peace in my heart."

I tell her, "I don't know what you've got in your heart, but it isn't peace from God. It's probably infatuation, but it is outside the revealed will of God."

It is never right to pray about that which God has already said is wrong. We might as well save our energy, because it isn't going to do any good. God doesn't change His mind. As far as I know, He hasn't written another Bible.

Prayer is not only motivated by the Word of God and measured by His will, but it is also manifested in our walk with God. Daniel not only prayed frequently, he also prayed fervently. He was committed to daily prayer; in fact, he prayed on his knees three times a day, whether he was busy with the affairs of state or whether the king issued a decree forbidding prayer to anyone except himself. When a crisis came, Daniel didn't change.

IS FERVENT PRAYER FANATICAL?

When Daniel prayed, he "turned to the Lord God and pleaded with him in prayer and petition, in fasting, and in sackcloth and ashes" (Dan. 9:3). This was a passionate prayer. It wasn't like ours, where we see God as a divine bellhop, getting us whatever we need at a moment's notice. We are told, "The effectual fervent prayer of a righteous man availeth much" (James 5:16 KJV).

Do we have any idea what it means to be fervent in prayer? If we think about the moment of our greatest crisis, whether it was physical, mental, or emotional, how did we pray? Did we say something like, "Lord, I have this need, and it sure would be neat if you could do something about it, but I don't want to take too much of your time. If you can do something, that would be great. Thanks, Lord." Or did we call out to God with such intensity that we almost ached?

In the Old Testament culture there were certain things that accompanied fervent prayer. First, in this passage from Daniel, he put on sackcloth, the garments of mourning. In the book of Job, it says that he prayed fervently while sitting in an ash pile and putting ashes on his head. It also says that praying fervently was accompanied by shaving off the hair of his head. In other places in the Bible we are told that praying was so agonizingly fervent that it was accompanied by crying, tearing clothes, fasting, sighing, groaning, and sweating blood. In our culture today, that sort of fervency would seem fanatical. We might be confronted by men in white coats carrying straitjackets. But I believe we have tilted in the opposite direction, presenting an emotionless, uninvolved relationship with Him.

When Daniel prayed fervently, he also fasted. What is the reason for this largely ignored practice of fasting?

IS FASTING FOR US?

We don't talk much about fasting today, but when we read the Bible there's something that really catches our attention. Jesus fasted. The apostle Paul fasted. In the Old Testament, Isaiah, Daniel, Esther, David, Hannah, Elijah, Ezra, Nehemiah, Zechariah, and others fasted. In church history we read that Martin Luther, John Calvin, John Knox, John and Charles Wesley, George Mueller, and many more fasted. We are not commanded to fast and we are not to do it as an outward expression of our piety, but there's no denying that sometimes fasting promotes fervency in our praying. It's a time in our lives when we say no to our physical wants and desires and prioritize the spiritual realm.

Reasons for fasting are varied. Sometimes in the Old Testament people fasted because of private problems. Hannah fasted because she had no children. Some fasted because of public disasters. In 1 Samuel 31 there is the story of Saul and his sons, including Jonathan, being killed in battle against the Philistines. The Israelites heard what the Philistines had done and fasted for seven days because of this tragedy. There were times when people fasted because of personal grief, as Queen Esther did when she heard the Jews were going to be killed. Sometimes fasting took place in penance over sin or because of compassion for friends. Other times those who fasted were searching for the will of God.

The New Testament teaches us that certain demons could not be cast out except by prayer and fasting. Paul fasted after his vision in Damascus, and again he fasted for fourteen days in a storm-tossed ship.

I have not told of these examples because I want all of us to start fasting. The point is that fasting is simply one measure of our fervency that is important in our relationship with God. I don't believe He is enamored with our cold, impersonal connection to Him. Sometimes that is the climate we experience in our churches today.

The story is told about a little monkey who got loose from an organ grinder on a cold winter day. The poor animal jumped onto the sill of a house. He looked through the window and saw a roaring fire. He found his way into the house and sat with his little paws raised to the fire. He froze to death, however, because his "fire" was a painted illustration on a fireplace screen.

There are churches and Christians who are like that. Painted fires on painted screens, with no emotion, no fervency, no warmth. Why do we wonder that people don't want to be part of a place like that? We only need to attend a World Series game or a championship basketball playoff to catch the enthusiasm of the fans. But when we come to church on Sunday, we seem to have the idea that we must stay jammed down in our skin like Ezekiel's dry bones.

I heard a pastor describe the unity in his church by saying, "Oh, yes, we're unified. In fact, if you want to know the truth, we're frozen together." Another pastor described his congregation by saying, "I'm sure that our church will go first in the Rapture because the Bible says, 'The dead in Christ will rise first.'"

I am not suggesting that we turn our churches into stadiums filled with frenzied fans, but if we really believe in the power of God, we need to pray with a little passion.

THREE OF THE HARDEST WORDS TO SAY

Some words stick in our throat. Among the hardest words to utter are "I have sinned." Life-changing prayer is borne out of confessing our wickedness before God. But what about Daniel? We learned when the governors and princes of Babylon sought to find a grievance against him, "They could find no corruption in him, because he was trustworthy and neither corrupt nor negligent" (Dan. 6:4). Daniel is one of a few men in the Old Testament about whom no evil word is written. But hear this prayer:

> O Lord, the great and awesome God, who keeps his covenant of love with all who love him and obey his commands, we have sinned and done wrong. We have been wicked and have rebelled; we have turned away from your commands and laws. We have not listened to your servants the prophets, who spoke in your name to our kings, our princes and our fathers, and to all the people of the land. (Dan. 9:4–6)

Daniel didn't point a finger and say, "Look, Lord, my people have really been wicked, and whatever you have done to them, they deserve it." No, he identified himself with the sin of his people and admitted to God that His judgment upon Israel for seventy years was just. This is one of the dynamic lessons of praying that I personally believe ought to be emulated today.

The Old Testament prophets always identified themselves with the sins of their people.

In the New Testament, especially in 1 Corinthians, we learn that as Christians we are one body. When one hurts, we all hurt. When one of us rejoices, we all rejoice. This may be a rather radical idea in our era of pointing fingers and condemning the sins of others, but I wonder what would happen if we pastors would stand in the pulpit on Sunday when there was known sin in the church and pray, "O God, we have committed adultery. O God, we have committed fornication. O God, we have been dishonest." Wouldn't that be a shocker?

One of the things I learned as a young pastor was that we are never right when we get into an I/Thou relationship with our congregation. What that means is that there is a difference between sharing in the teaching of the Word of God and being preached at. The preacher who preaches at you says, "If *you* don't watch out, this is what is going to happen to *you. You* better get *your* life straightened out, and if *you* don't, *you're* headed for a fall."

The biblical style is that the preacher doesn't set himself apart from the temptations and the sin. He should be saying, "There's not anything that you are capable of doing that I am not capable of doing. We are in this together, and not one of us can sin without it affecting the other." Until we can get, as Daniel did, a sense of corporate guilt before God, we will never have holiness within the church as God wants us to have.

Now, it's true that there was no sin recorded of Daniel, but obviously he was a sinner. He was a very righteous, holy man. Compared to our holiness today, he was a cut above the average. Why would he confess his sin? The more devout a person is, the deeper his love for God and commitment to Christ, the greater will be his sense of sinfulness.

Someone once told me the meaning of the church steeple. Supposedly it teaches us that the closer you get to God, the smaller you are. That is the reason why Daniel calls out to God in confession of sin, not because he was such a great sinner, but because he was walking with God in such close fellowship that even the incidental sins of his own life were magnified in his mind and heart.

THE PAIN OF CONFESSION

In the New Testament, the word *confession* means "to admit our guilt." When we confess our sins we verbalize our spiritual shortcomings. There's a tremendous amount of pain in confession. I've tried to understand why, and I think I have some clues.

Perhaps when we confess we recognize that we have a responsibility to change what it is we have told God we are doing. When we come to God we say, "Lord, I have sinned by . . . (you fill in your blanks; I have my own)." Implicit in that confession is that we're not going to do it anymore. Many times we try to hang on to every pet sin in our lives. E. M. Blaiklock, who has written a great deal about prayer, said, "This period of our devotions must contain a moment of pain. It is not God's intention that we should writhe under it, or linger in it. But specific and sincere confession of our own sin is no joyous exercise."[1]

If you are married, the hardest words to say seem to be, "Honey, I was wrong." For instance, when you're traveling down the highway with your wife and she tells you that you should have turned. You say, "I know where I'm going. That's not the way." All of a sudden you realize in your heart that you should have turned. Do you know how far a man will drive to keep his wife from knowing that she was right and he was wrong? (I speak from experience.) It would be so much simpler to pull over to the side of the road and say, "Honey, I was wrong."

If we can understand that in terms of our personal relationships, then we can understand why it is so hard for us to come to God and say, "God, I was wrong, and I confess my sin."

A SPIRITUAL MAGNIFYING GLASS

Life-changing prayer magnifies the Lord. The Greek word for *magnify* means "to make great." When Daniel prayed, he placed a spiritual magnifying glass over the attributes of God. He said, "O Lord, the great and awesome God." "Lord, You are righteous." "O Lord our God, who brought Your people out of Egypt with a mighty hand." "We do not make requests of You because we are righteous, but because of Your great mercy."

Does God need for us to tell Him these things? Surely not. But God needs to hear us say them so that He knows we know them. We cannot praise God and be self-centered. One cannot praise God without relinquishing his occupation with himself.

Someone told me that if you want to get in good with God, just brag on His Son. Magnify and glorify the Lord Jesus Christ.

When Daniel was magnifying and glorifying God, he came to the end of the prayer with a tremendous truth. What was the motivation and purpose behind his prayer? He certainly wasn't praying for his own safety. He had very few years left to live, and leaving captivity—going back to Jerusalem where there was a lot of hard work to restore the city, the walls, the temple, where everything was in ruin—didn't mean very much to him. His driving motivation was for God to restore His people to their city, their sanctuary, and their culture.

The whole character of his prayer is wrapped up in this verse: "O Lord, in keeping with all your righteous acts, turn away your anger and your wrath from Jerusalem, your city, your holy hill. Our sins and the iniquities of our fathers have made Jerusalem and your people an object of scorn to all those around us" (Dan. 9:16).

Daniel went to God and said, "God, everybody is talking about us as Your people. They are saying that You have forgotten us. God, for Your own glory and honor, for the sake of Your worth, I beg of You, restore us to the place of honor we once knew."

How do we pray? Most of our prayers are so self-centered that we have no time to be God-centered. What would happen to us if we would get caught up in the fact that we are Christians? We bear the name of Christ in how we live and what we do. We carry God's reputation into the community wherever we go. If we followed Daniel's example, jealous for God's reputation and for His testimony, what a difference it would make in the way we live and the manner in which we pray.

It takes a long, long time to learn what prayer can do in one's life. We stumble around and try to use the right words and the proper thoughts, but somehow they sound hollow to us. So often we have thought prayer was getting God to bless whatever we were doing or what we wanted to do. But real prayer is finding out what God is doing and asking Him to help us know what He wants us to do.

In the past I have loved water skiing. I learned if I stayed in the wake of the boat, it was easy. When I decided to get outside the wake, out where the pros are jumping waves, it can get pretty hairy. Most of the time I spent getting back on the skis. But if I stayed in the wake, I could go for miles and not have any problems.

Prayer is finding out where the boat is going and staying in the wake. It is finding out what God is doing, asking Him to help us know what He wants us to do, and then focusing in on it.

In my own life I am constantly asking God, "What do You want me to do?" When we get away from all the things we are doing and focus on what God is doing, then we can have His blessing.

When Daniel found the will of God, he began to pray fervently for its accomplishment. The reason he was so concerned about sin was because it was a barrier to knowing what God was doing. So prayer is really a matter of coming to God and being totally submissive to Him in body, soul, and spirit.

This story about Dwight L. Moody has been a real challenge to me. In 1872, Moody attended an early-morning meeting in a hay mow in Ireland. He heard a man quietly say, "The world has yet to see what God can do with, and for, and through, and in a man who is fully and wholly consecrated to God's will." Moody would later say "those were the words sent to my soul . . . from the Living God. As I crossed the wide Atlantic, the boards of the deck of the vessel were engraved with them, and when I reached Chicago, the very paving stones seemed marked with 'Moody, the world has yet to see what God will do with a man fully consecrated to him.'"[2]

God honored Moody with a ministry that, in spite of his human frailties and lack of formal education, has touched lives even until this day. Moody found out what God was doing and got in on it.

I struggle with all the humanistic ideas that come my way, the "Seven Easy Steps to Be Successful," and other self-help themes. God just keeps saying over and over again, "Jeremiah, all I want you to do is find out what I am doing and get in on it."

ANSWER TO DANIEL'S PRAYER

When Daniel finished his fervent prayer, the answer came to him through God's special messenger. That answer is the backbone of all prophecy. Beginning five centuries before the birth of Christ, told to a man who was totally committed to God, we are given the privilege of seeing the panorama of history until the end times.

The seventy weeks of Daniel are literally the key to the prophetic word. How grateful I am to this man for preserving the words of God, delivered by the angel Gabriel so we could understand them in this crucial period of our planet's existence.

15

UNLOCKING THE
PROPHETIC WORD

L eopold Cohn, a European rabbi, studied the prophecy of the seventy weeks of Daniel 9 and, on the basis of verses 25 and 26, came
to the conclusion that the Messiah had already come. Puzzled by this,
he approached an older rabbi and asked, "Where is the Messiah?"

The rabbi didn't know the answer but told him he thought the
Messiah was in New York City. So Cohn sold almost everything he
owned and bought a passage to America, seeking the Messiah. He
arrived in New York and began to wander up and down the streets,
looking for the Messiah. One night he walked past the door of a gospel
mission and heard people singing. He went in, sat down in the back of
the room and heard a preacher talk about Jesus Christ, the Messiah.
That night Leopold Cohn received this same Jesus as his Savior.

Soon after, Cohn bought a stable, swept it out, set up some
chairs, and began to hold his own gospel meetings. That was the
first outreach of what was to become Chosen People Ministries. It
all started because a rabbi read the ninth chapter of Daniel.[1]

Sir Isaac Newton said that at about the time of the end there would be a body of men who would turn their attention to the prophecies of the Word of God, and they would insist upon their literal interpretation in the midst of much clamor and resistance. I believe we are living in that time. Newton also said we could stake the truth of Christianity on this prophecy alone, because five centuries before Christ was born, His coming was foretold.[2]

The interesting fact about the seventy weeks of Daniel, which is the prophecy, is that sixty-nine seventieths of it have already been fulfilled. We can go back into history and trace the literal, detailed fulfillment of the sixty-nine weeks. This gives us complete confidence to believe that what God has done in the first part of the prophecy, He will surely do in the last part.

SECRET OF THE PROPHECY

This prophecy is the answer to Daniel's prayer. God chose to answer him with a revelation about the future that no one to that time had received. While Daniel was deeply engrossed in prayer, Gabriel arrived after a fast flight from heaven. The angel touched him on the shoulder and said, "You called?"

> While I was still in prayer, Gabriel, the man I had seen in the earlier vision, came to me in swift flight about the time of the evening sacrifice. (Dan. 9:21)

Some people think angels are omnipresent, but they are not. They cannot be everywhere at once; they have to move in space. Daniel was on his knees when God said to Gabriel, "Look, I want you to go down there and give Daniel some information, and I want you to go right now." The order was given as soon as Daniel started to pray, so Gabriel's trip was at high speed.

When Gabriel showed up, the message was red-letter important! He is the one who told Mary about Jesus. He is the one who told Zacharias about John. When Daniel looked around and saw Gabriel, recognizing the man who had interpreted the vision of the ram and the goat, he knew something great was going to happen.

Gabriel said, "Daniel, I have now come to give you insight and understanding. As soon as you began to pray, an answer was given, which I have come to tell you, for you are highly esteemed (Dan. 9:22–23).

In the King James Version, it says, "thou art greatly beloved." It is significant that the greatest source of prophetic information in the New Testament is the apostle John, and Daniel is the leading prophet in the Old Testament. Both of them are described as "greatly beloved." The secret of God giving Daniel and John the special privilege of being the bearers of prophetic revelation is in their unusual obedience to God.

MAKING SENSE OUT OF NUMBERS

Gabriel begins his message with some numbers that are vitally important for us to understand. He tells Daniel, "Seventy 'sevens' are decreed for your people." Another version says "seventy weeks." Most of us know what a week is, but if we think this means a week of days, it won't work. In the Old Testament, the week refers to seven years, not seven days.

One proof of this is in Leviticus where it says, "For six years sow your fields, and for six years prune your vineyards and gather their crops. But in the seventh year the land is to have a sabbath of rest, a sabbath to the LORD" (Lev. 25:3–4). We know about the Sabbath day, but here the Bible teaches us about the Sabbath year. The Jewish people were told to count off seven sabbaths of years (seven times seven years), and then there was to be the year of Jubilee. The week of years was a part of the Old Testament culture, so Daniel must have been mentally calculating the time frame Gabriel gave him.

The prophecy of the seventy weeks has to do with 490 years. Until this time, we have seen God's prophecies concerning the Gentile rulers and nations. Now He says, "I haven't forgotten you, Jewish people. I have cut out of the calendar 490 years that belong to you, and I'm going to show you how my program is going to work in that period of time."

If weeks are years, how long is a year? Most of us would answer, "A year is 365 days, of course." No, it isn't. In the Old Testament, the prophetic year was 360 days long. The account of the Genesis flood gives us the mathematical reasoning behind the days in the year.

In Genesis 7 and 8 we are told that the flood began on the seventeenth day of the second month and ended on the seventeenth day of the seventh month. So, the flood lasted for five months, didn't it? In the same chapter it says the waters flooded the earth for 150 days. Simple division will show us that the months were 30 days in duration, and 12 months times 30 days equals 360 days, which was the length of the Jewish year.

Scholars such as Sir Robert Anderson and Harold Hoehner have converted the 360-day Jewish calendar into our 365-day calendar, and when all of the information was inserted into the equation the conclusion was the same. Perhaps you are thinking, "What happened to the other five days?" We don't have a perfect calendar, so we have what we call leap year. The Jews did the same thing, which we'll find out about later. However, their leap year was a bigger leap than ours.

PEOPLE OF PROPHECY

This is a prophecy concerning the Jewish people and their holy city. God is basically saying, "Look, Daniel, I am not finished with your people yet. I have a plan for you and I want to tell you how this fits in with my plan for the Gentiles."

God tells Daniel six things that are going to happen to the Jews:

Seventy "sevens" are decreed for your people and your holy city to finish transgression, to put an end to sin, to atone for wickedness, to bring in everlasting righteousness, to seal up vision and prophecy and to anoint the most holy. (Dan. 9:24)

Daniel had confessed his sin and the sin of his people, and now God says, "Daniel, one of these days I am going to put an end to sin and wickedness. I've got a plan for you and your people that is overwhelming. I am going to bring in righteousness and anoint the holy place. You're going to know the end of my plan for the Jews."

We may have forgotten that God's plan for the Jews has never abated. Neither the events of the past nor the persecution of our day has changed God's plan. Today we are living in an era when God's time clock of 490 years has been temporarily interrupted. We are at a little stopping-off place, a parenthesis in His story.

ISRAEL, TEMPORARILY SIDETRACKED

The Jews are God's chosen people. When He sent the Lord Jesus into this world, I believe He literally offered Himself to His people. The Bible says, "He came unto his own, and his own received him not. But as many as received him, to them gave He power to become the sons of God" (John 1:11–12 KJV). When Israel rejected Jesus as its Messiah, He turned to the Gentiles and He put aside His plan for the Jews.

Dr. Louis Talbot, the founder of Talbot Seminary, said that one day he was on a train and all of a sudden it came to a stop. He asked the conductor what had happened and was told, "We're on a side-track. The express is coming, and we had to get off so it could come through."

Dr. Talbot said that's exactly what's happened to the nation of Israel. They were on the main line, but they rejected their Messiah. So God placed them on the sideline as a nation. He still calls out to individual Jewish people, but the Gospel Express, which we know as the church, is going through.

We are living now on that express, in the parentheses of time before Israel gets back on the track. I believe we are right at the end of the parenthetic section, and that soon the Rapture is going to happen. Then the Tribulation, which we know as the seventieth week of Daniel, will be ushered in.

HOW THIS ALL FITS TOGETHER

To the person who is serious about studying the Word of God, this prophecy is an exciting blessing. Here is God, centuries before His work, telling His prophet Daniel what He is going to do.

When the critics come to the book of Daniel, they hate the ninth chapter because it is prewritten history. We are going to see that God predicted the time when the prophecy would start. He predicted the very day when Jesus would ride into the city in His triumphal entry and the time of the destruction of Jerusalem. The only way the critics can attack the historical accuracy of these predictions is to play the game of late dating. The rules of that game are to say, "I don't believe in predictive prophecy, I don't think anybody can tell us what happens before it happens, so the book was obviously written after the fact." This is called "higher criticism" for some unknown reason.

The easiest way to understand the entire prophecy is to see that verse 24 is a summary of the prophecy. Then verse 25 gives us information about the first sixty-nine weeks of Daniel's seventy weeks:

> Know and understand this: From the issuing of the decree to restore and rebuild Jerusalem until the Anointed One, the ruler, comes, there will be seven "sevens." It will be rebuilt with streets and a trench, but in times of trouble.

The next verse gives us the picture of the time we are in now—that sidetrack we are on:

> After the sixty-two "sevens," the Anointed One will be cut off and will have nothing. The people of the ruler who will come will destroy the city and the sanctuary. The end will come like a flood: War will continue until the end, and desolations have been decreed.

The last verse in chapter 9 is the seventieth week of Daniel, which is where we'll see another view of the infamous Dark Prince.

THE JEWS ARE STILL WAITING

Two Christians were examining a model of first-century Jerusalem at the Holy Land Hotel in Jerusalem. The model was beautifully constructed, using, as far as possible, the original materials of the time: marble, stone, wood, copper, and iron. The two men were discussing the future rebuilding of the temple, and a stranger standing nearby overheard their conversation. He introduced himself as a rabbi from New York and said, "May I ask you a question? Do Christians really believe in the rebuilding of the temple in Jerusalem?"

One of the Christians answered, "But, Rabbi, haven't you read your own prophets, Ezekiel and Daniel?"

The rabbi said, "No, as a matter of fact I haven't. When I was studying to be a rabbi I was told not to read Daniel."

This rabbi did not seem to have the choice to examine the Scripture that Leopold Cohn did, because if he had read Daniel 9 he would have discovered that the Messiah had already come. Many Jews are still waiting for Him.

As Christians, we are not looking for Him to come the first time; we are looking for His return.

16

NO WONDER
JESUS WEPT

Some things are very hard to understand. Take the handwriting of a doctor, for instance. I heard about a patient who went to a doctor for a checkup and was given a slip of paper with a prescription. The patient put it in his pocket and forgot to have it filled. However, every morning for two years he showed it to the conductor as a railroad pass. Twice it got him into Radio City Music Hall, and one time he showed it at the door and was allowed into the symphony. He got a raise from Human Resources by showing it as a note from his boss. One day he mislaid it at home, and his daughter picked it up, played it on the piano, and won a scholarship to the conservatory of music.

Some may say the prophecy of the seventy weeks of Daniel is just as outlandish as that story and just as illegible as the handwriting. However, this prophecy was not written to confuse us but to allow us to understand the end from the beginning of God's wonderful plan for His people, the Jews.

THE FIRST SIXTY-NINE YEARS

Daniel 9:25 states that the starting point of the seventy weeks is the issuance of a command to restore and rebuild Jerusalem. Daniel was told by the angel, "Know and understand this: From the issuing of the decree to restore and rebuild Jerusalem until the Anointed One, the ruler, comes, there will be seven 'sevens' and sixty-two 'sevens.' It will be rebuilt with streets and a trench, but in times of trouble."

Daniel was told that the entire city would be rebuilt, including the great open court within the walls. Can you imagine the thrill in his heart to hear that the city of his boyhood, the place of his birth, which had been turned to rubble by the Babylonian invasion, would be rebuilt? The timing is the important part.

To start God's time clock again, we need to look at Nehemiah 2. Nehemiah was a man of great faith and prayer who led the third return of the exiles to Jerusalem. Two major expeditions had already made the long journey after Cyrus had given them their freedom.

Nehemiah was the chief butler of King Artaxerxes. His duties of selecting and tasting the king's wine gave him constant access to the throne. One day he brought the wine into the royal chambers, and the king took one look at him and said, "Nehemiah, you look terrible. If you're not sick, what's gotten into you?"

Here was Nehemiah's big chance. He put the tray down, said a silent prayer, and launched into his request.

"Your majesty, I'm very sad because the city where my ancestors are buried is in ruins. Even the gates of the city have been burned to the ground."

The king stroked his beard, looked at Nehemiah, and wondered what he wanted. Nehemiah became bolder. "King, if I have served you well, here's my request. Send me to Judah, to the city of Jerusalem, and let me rebuild the city."

Artaxerxes turned to his wife and got a little nod of approval. Even kings want their wives around to approve of their decisions. "Tell me, Nehemiah, how long will you be gone and when will you come back?"

Nehemiah was prepared and gave the king a definite time schedule, and then forged ahead with a list of supplies he would need. Artaxerxes issued a decree for the city to be rebuilt, and without realizing it, began the exact fulfillment of prophecy.

In Nehemiah 2:1, it says: "In the month of Nisan in the twentieth year of King Artaxerxes . . . ." This was the date Nehemiah made his request and the king issued the decree. Now, for those who enjoy working riddles, this should be easy. Artaxerxes began to reign in 465 BC and so the twentieth year of his reign would have been 445 BC. (Remember, we count backwards in the BC years.) The first day of Nisan is March 14, according to our calendar, recognizing that our months are not contiguous with theirs. Now we are getting close to the specific time when the first sixty-nine weeks of Daniel will begin.

According to Nehemiah 2:1–8, the first sixty-nine weeks began at a specific time, 445 BC, and ended at a certain time and event. The sixty-nine weeks of Daniel began with March 14, 445 BC, when Artaxerxes' decree went forth.

We need to remember that weeks are counted as years, and the years had 360 days. Simple calculation of this time element is this: 69 weeks (of years) x 7 (days in the week) = 483 x 360 (days in the year) = 173,880. Now if you take March 14, 445 BC, when the decree to rebuild Jerusalem went forth, and add to it 173,880 days, you come to April 6, AD 32. According to Sir Robert Anderson in his chronology, it was on *that day that Jesus Christ rode into the city in His triumphal entry.*

Gabriel told Daniel that from the moment the decree went forth to rebuild the city until the Anointed One—the ruler, or Messiah the Prince—would come, that an exact number of years would pass. God's special agent had accurate instructions; there was no communication gap.

THE DAY THIS PROPHECY CAME TRUE

It was a day unlike any day that ever took place up to that time. The Savior had sent His disciples to find a certain colt upon which He must ride. Whoever heard of a king riding on a donkey? Yet Zechariah the prophet foretold hundreds of years before that this is exactly the manner of transportation the Messiah would use.

The people shouted hosannas and waved palms to celebrate His coming. The disciples were praising God for all the miracles they had seen. After all, they had walked with Him and stood in awe as He healed the sick and raised the dead. But they had been told by their Master to tell no one. Jesus had refused to allow His disciples to make Him known as the Messiah. But on this day, something was happening. Some of the people were saying, "You should rebuke your disciples, because they're calling you the Messiah." What did Jesus say?

"'I tell you,' he replied, 'if they keep quiet, the stones will cry out'" (Luke 19:40).

No keeping quiet about the Messiah that day! This was the day Jesus was to come forth, just as Daniel had prophesied. While the people were singing and praising Him, Jesus had an unusual reaction. Instead of being pleased with this tremendous reception, He wept. For a long time I didn't understand this, until I began to study again the book of Daniel. Jesus said,

> If you, even you, had only known on this day what would bring you peace—but now it is hidden from your eyes. The days will come upon you when your enemies will build an embankment against

you and encircle you and hem you in on every side. They will dash you to the ground, you and the children within your walls. They will not leave one stone on another, *because you did not recognize the time of God's coming to you.* (Luke 19:42–44, emphasis added)

No wonder Jesus wept. He had dispatched His holy messenger 483 years earlier to His beloved prophet, Daniel, and told him the exact moment when Messiah the Prince would be proclaimed. But there wasn't a single person who understood enough of the Old Testament to recognize that this was His day. The Bible says, "He came to that which was his own, but his own did not receive him. Yet to all who received him, to those who believed in his name, he gave the right to become children of God" (John 1:11–12).

The prophecy says that after the Anointed One came, He "will be cut off." It wasn't but a few days after His triumphal entrance into Jerusalem that Jesus was crucified, fulfilling the last part of verse 25.

Because His people didn't know Him, Jesus turned from His program for the Jews and initiated His plan for the Gentiles. We have learned that God's program for Israel encompassed 490 years. Since 483 years had passed, it's obvious that there were seven years left. Between the crucifixion and the last seven years is an undated period of time. We're living in that gap today.

UNDERSTANDING THE GAP

When Daniel was told that six things were to happen to complete the prophecy of seventy weeks, Gabriel listed them:

1. finish transgression
2. put an end to sin
3. atone for wickedness

4. bring in everlasting righteousness
5. seal up vision and prophecy
6. anoint the most holy.

Have those things occurred? Is there everlasting peace in Israel? Is the temple, the holy place, anointed? In fact, is there a temple to anoint? Is there still sin in the world? We all know that none of these prophecies have been fulfilled.

Gabriel further said to Daniel, "The people of the ruler who will come will destroy the city and the sanctuary" (Dan. 9:26). In AD 70, Jerusalem was destroyed, almost forty years after the death of Christ. The entire civilization of the Jews ceased to exist and that desolation continued until recent times.

The Old Testament prophets did not see things as we do today. We look at years coming one after another. (The older we get the faster they go.) The prophets of old—Daniel, Isaiah, Jeremiah, and others—looked into the future and saw all of the things God was going to do through His Son, the Messiah, but His coming the first time and His Second Advent merged together. The Rapture wasn't even mentioned in the Old Testament.

The familiar Christmas passage from Isaiah illustrates this two-fold prophecy. "For unto us a child is born, unto us a son is given." This happened when Jesus came into this world the first time. But here is the rest of the verse: "and the government shall be upon his shoulder: and his name shall be called Wonderful, Counsellor, The mighty God, The everlasting Father, The Prince of Peace" (Isa. 9:6 KJV). When Jesus came the first time, was the government upon His shoulder? Certainly not. The government nailed Him to a cross. When He comes the second time, He will be the government. In the same verse, the prophecy jumps two thousand years or more. But Isaiah saw it all in one view.

Another prophet who had a double prophecy was Zechariah. "Rejoice greatly, O Daughter of Zion! Shout, Daughter of Jerusalem! See, your king comes to you, righteous and having salvation, gentle and riding on a donkey" (Zech. 9:9). We have just discovered when that happened. But the next verse is: "I will take away the chariots from Ephraim and the war-horses from Jerusalem, and the battle bow will be broken. He will proclaim peace to the nations. His rule will extend from sea to sea and from the River to the ends of the earth" (Zech. 9:10). Nothing like that happened when Jesus walked on earth. Once again, a prophet looked into the future.

THE END OF THE SIXTY-NINE WEEKS

With the end of the 483 years, it was time for the church to move in, based on Acts 2 and the coming of the Holy Spirit. Daniel doesn't say anything about that because he didn't know anything about it. The church is a mystery in the Old Testament.

During this gap, the church is growing, adding new members, and working to restrain the complete onslaught of evil in the world. At the end of the church age, Jesus Christ is coming for His own, and the church will be raptured out of this world.

With all the Christians gone, planet Earth will become a hotbed of insurrection and hatred. The scene will be set for a strong leader to arrive with a promise to return order and offer a solution for economic problems.

BROKEN PROMISES, BROKEN PEOPLE

By this time, Daniel must have been overwhelmed by Gabriel's words. As the seventy weeks unfold, he was then given a small window into the last week of years.

He will confirm a covenant with many for one "seven." In the middle of the "seven" he will put an end to sacrifice and offering. And on a wing of the temple he will set up an abomination that causes desolation, until the end that is decreed is poured out on him. (Dan. 9:27)

This is the "ruler who will come," mentioned in verse 26. He is the little horn of Daniel 7, the king of fierce countenance, the man of sin, the beast, and all of those other names that we have for the Antichrist. We have many antichrists in the world today, but none who have the demonic qualities of this man. One of his first acts of leadership will be to make a treaty with the Jewish people. More than anything else in the world, the Jews long for the restoration of their temple and the temple sacrifice. One day there is going to be this great leader who will sit down at a conference table and say, "My dear friends, it's my desire to help you restore your religious heritage. I have the resources and manpower to rebuild your glorious temple."

The Jewish leaders will be duped into believing that this man is sincere, and they will agree to anything he demands. Only three and a half years later, the Antichrist will tear up his agreement like a meaningless piece of paper. The temple itself will be so desecrated that it will no longer be regarded as the temple of the Lord, but as an idol temple. What Antiochus did in a small way in the second century BC will become a worldwide persecution of Israel.

The last three and a half years of time will be bathed in blood. According to some reports in the Scriptures, blood will flow as high as the bridles of horses and corpses will produce such a terrible smell that ships passing in the harbor will try to divert their travel so they do not have to pass by the destruction.

Jesus prophesied about this time of great tribulation:

So when you see standing in the holy place "the abomination that causes desolation," spoken of through the prophet Daniel—let the reader understand—then let those who are in Judea flee to the mountains. Let no one on the roof of his house go down to take anything out of the house. Let no one in the field go back to get his cloak. How dreadful it will be in those days for pregnant women and nursing mothers! Pray that your flight will not take place in winter or on the Sabbath. For then there will be great distress, unequaled from the beginning of the world until now—and never to be equaled again. If those days had not been cut short, no one would survive, but for the sake of the elect those days will be shortened. (Matt. 24:15–22)

Take all of the horrors of war that you can imagine, multiply them a thousand times, and you have not approached the awful holocaust that will take place during the last half of the Tribulation period.

At the end of the seventieth week, Christ the King shall come, and Scripture says that all Israel will be saved. The Scripture says that Israel will be reconciled to their Messiah and their rebellion will be over. Daniel was told that at the end of the 490 years, God would establish His program for the Jews and everlasting righteousness would reign. A glorious temple will be rebuilt, where worship can be carried on by the Jews. It will be a temple unlike any that has ever existed.

SEVENTY WEEKS OUT OF EONS OF TIME

When my children were in school, at times they would question why they had to study certain required subjects which did not appear to have any useful purpose. "To get good grades so you can get into college" may not have been a very sharp answer. But when it comes to studying the cryptic seventy weeks in Daniel, I think there are some good reasons why it is important.

First, the prophecy teaches us that God hasn't forgotten His people, the Jews. Imagine how Daniel felt—a captive for sixty-nine years, sitting there in that Babylonian culture which had been taken over by the Persians, and wondering, "Has God forsaken us?" In answer to his prayer, God said He hadn't forgotten His promises. Someone has said that the king of Egypt couldn't diminish the Jew; the waters of the Red Sea could not drown him; Balaam couldn't curse him; the fiery furnace couldn't devour him; the gallows of Haman couldn't hang him; nations couldn't assimilate him; and dictators couldn't annihilate him. No matter where we go today we see the various cultures and races of the world assimilated into one another. But that is not true of the Jews. There are Russian Jews, German Jews, Polish Jews, and American Jews. God has preserved their unique identity because one day His plan for His chosen people is going to be fulfilled.

Second, there was a purpose of the captivity. In the 490 years before that captivity, the Jews had violated their Sabbath. God had told them to set aside one year out of seven as holy for Him, but they had refused. So God said, "If you will not give me the Sabbath years, I will take them from you." So for seventy years He took the Jews out of their land, and it was desolated. He took His Sabbath years because the Jews wouldn't give them to Him willingly.

After He had the seventy years back from the Jews, He said, "Now, I have 490 more years I want to tell you about that are yet out in the future."

During the seventy years of captivity, some positive things happened to the Jews.

While the Jews were in Babylon, something was born into their culture called synagogues. They couldn't worship at their temple, so the rabbis decided to teach them in a type of house church. Out of the synagogue came the roots of the churches of today. It was just a slight transition from the synagogues to the individual churches of Christianity.

While the Jews were in captivity, the Old Testament canon of the Bible was completed. In fact, the earliest record we have of a collection of Old Testament books is that which took place under the leadership of Ezra following the seventy years of captivity. When we open our Bibles today and leaf through the books of the Old Testament, we know they began with a collection of scrolls in Babylon. Out of Babylon came many beneficial results.

There are many times when I don't know what God is doing with me. *What in the world is going on in my life? Lord, why have you put me in this situation?* I have learned over the years that God was at work even when I didn't understand what He was doing.

We can also learn that He is a personal God. On several occasions in the life of Daniel, who was greatly loved of the Lord because of his obedience, God touched him. He touched him to make him speak, to give him skill, when he needed to stand, and when he needed to be strong. God cares about His people.

TEARS OF GOD

Jesus saw the future when he rode into Jerusalem on a donkey. Not only the carnage that was to destroy the city, but also the time of terror that would come for all who rejected Him. And He wept.

Tears come easily for me. When I try to place myself in the sandals of a prophet like Daniel, I become overwhelmed with the knowledge God gave him. It motivates me when I realize there are many people who do not understand what these prophecies mean to their own future.

No wonder Jesus wept, for He knew there would be those who scoffed, doubted, and ignored His chosen servants. But how exciting it is to be a part of the vast and growing army of believers who take these prophecies seriously.

DEMON POWER

If you have ever had a child who has rebelled and rejected your moral teaching, or a friend who betrayed your trust, you may have a slight understanding of the agony surging through Daniel's spirit. While he was experiencing a great personal conflict on earth, another conflict was being waged in the heavens.

The tenth chapter of Daniel prepares us for the final vision God gives to His servant and the startling scenario of the end times. The time is the third year of the reign of Cyrus the Persian. It has been just two years since the decree was given for the Jews to return to their homeland and begin to rebuild the temple in Jerusalem. Cyrus, with kingly generosity, proclaimed that any Jew who wanted to go back could do so. What a time! There must have been dancing on the walls of the city and parades beneath the Ishtar Gate. Daniel should have been a contented old man, living out his years in peaceful retirement. The madness of Nebuchadnezzar, the threat of the lions' den, and the visions of the Antichrist were enough challenges for a lifetime. The captivity was over; his people were free. But the old prophet, with a mind as sharp as it was when he entered Nebuchadnezzar's court seventy years before, was deeply burdened.

MY PEOPLE, MY PEOPLE

Daniel 10:1 says: "In the third year of Cyrus king of Persia, a revelation was given to Daniel (who was called Belteshazzar). Its message was true and it concerned a great war. The understanding of the message came to him in a vision."

One part of the "great war" was the turmoil in Daniel's heart. Although they had been freed, there were still many Jews left in Babylon. Surprising as it may seem, less than fifty thousand people volunteered to return to Israel. There were many Jews who were still living as aliens in a land of idols. Daniel must have thought he was too old to return or that the remaining Jews needed him in Babylon, but the fact that there were still thousands of able-bodied people content to be displaced persons was troubling.

The news from Jerusalem was also disturbing. The small remnant of Jews who had returned weren't working very hard. It took them two years just to get the foundation of the temple started. In addition, some renegade Jews who lived in that territory decided they were going to give the builders a hard time. The fourth chapter of Ezra records how the enemies of Judah did everything they could to discourage the builders. Finally, an edict was sent out to stop all the reconstruction work. The word filtered back to Daniel via camel express, and he also heard that his people had fallen back into the same kinds of sins that put them into captivity in the first place.

"At that time I, Daniel, mourned for three weeks. I ate no choice food; no meat or wine touched my lips; and I used no lotions at all until the three weeks were over" (Dan. 10:2–3).

He fasted, stayed inside, and didn't anoint his body. It was the custom of the Jews to use some sort of a lotion on their bodies when they were in a joyous frame of mind. It was rather like slapping on some aftershave or cologne before going out in public. When Daniel was burdened he didn't go to a counselor, complain to his friends, or gripe to his neighbors. Daniel went right to the source. He prayed.

As I have looked back over my life, I discovered that I have some terrible temptations when I am troubled. I want to find a friend who will listen to me. I believe all of us need someone we can pour out our hearts to, but isn't it interesting that we do everything except the one thing God has provided for us when we are down?

I remember reading the story of Andrew Bonar, one of the great preachers and writers of the last century. His daughter was taking a Welsh evangelist through the church her father pastored. She said:

> When I was a little girl, my daddy used to bring me here and tell me to sit in a pew in the back. He would say, "I'll be back in a little while. You stay here."
>
> He'd leave me, and I wouldn't see him for a while. One day, I decided to find out what he was doing, so I crawled out of the pew and walked up the aisle until I finally found him. I saw the strangest thing. My dad would be seated in a pew, bent forward as if to read the name on the plaque. [In those days it was common to put names on each pew.] He would read the name and bow his head and pray. Then he would scoot over and read the name on the next pew and pray again. My father would spend an entire evening in the place where the people of God came to worship and, one by one, pray for every parishioner in his church. He had an overwhelming burden for his people.[1]

I wonder what would happen if those of us in the ministry would carry the burdens that God places on our hearts back to the source, even as Daniel did.

Some people like to get outside and walk when they are troubled. When we leave our natural environment we seem to be able to think better, to look at our problems with a different perspective. After three weeks of prayer and fasting, Daniel went for a stroll along the river with some friends. His prayers had some potency, for they got the attention of the angels. God sent one of His special emissaries to Daniel, like the one the apostle John described in the first chapter of Revelation.

Imagine strolling by the river, skipping a stone now and then across the water, and all of a sudden seeing this brilliant figure: "I looked up and there before me was a man dressed in linen, with a belt of the finest gold around his waist. His body was like chrysolite, his face like lightning, his eyes like flaming torches, his arms and legs like the gleam of burnished bronze, and his voice like the sound of a multitude" (Dan. 10:5–6).

Daniel's friends stood with blank faces, seeing nothing. But something in the atmosphere terrified them so much that they turned on their heels and hid behind the bushes. Our brave friend did the next natural thing. He passed out cold.

It took the angel some doing to get Daniel to the point where he was clearheaded enough to understand what God wanted to communicate to him. First the angel reached out and touched him, then helped him get on his hands and knees. He was trembling so hard that the angel said, "Daniel, you are greatly loved by God and He has sent me with an important message. Stand up and listen to me."

Daniel stood up, shaky and deathly pale, teetering on the edge of collapse at any moment. He steadied himself and looked into the face of this holy messenger. God does answer prayers in some astounding ways! When he had previously prayed fervently, his prayers were answered before they were out of his mouth. This time, he had been praying for three weeks with no response, until suddenly this shining person appeared. Daniel wasn't accustomed to such slow service. I can imagine him thinking, *Where have you been all this time? I'm almost starved.*

Some people believe this angel was an appearance of Jesus in the Old Testament. Theologically, this is called a christophany, or theophany. At one time I thought this was true, because it sounds like the picture of Jesus in Revelation. But I have come to believe it wasn't the Lord, because the Scripture says that the one who came down withstood one of Satan's emissaries for twenty-one days. My Lord isn't like that. I doubt if He has ever been detained by one of Satan's cohorts, even though the Spirit of God took Him to the wilderness and Satan tempted Him for forty days.

I believe God chose one of his top ambassadors to bring this message to Daniel. No lower-echelon worker would do.

BATTLEGROUND IN THE HEAVENLIES

God heard Daniel from the moment he started to pray, but the answer was intercepted somewhere between heaven and earth. With Daniel shaking in his sandals in front of him, the angel said:

> Do not be afraid, Daniel. Since the first day that you set your mind to gain understanding and to humble yourself before your God, your words were heard, and I have come in response to them. But the prince of the Persian kingdom resisted me twenty-one days. Then Michael, one of the chief princes, came to help me, because I was detained there with the king of Persia. (Dan. 10:12–13)

This is a fascinating account. Daniel was praying on earth. God heard in heaven and dispatched an angel with a special delivery answer. However, between heaven and earth that angel was accosted by an evil angel, a demon, and a battle took place. After three weeks of warfare, God's angel, with the help of Michael, one of the chief princes, shook off the bandit and continued his journey to earth.

You may be thinking, *That is the most bizarre thing I've ever heard. What science fiction book have you been reading?* This is not a fictional story. Satan does have his angels, and they are very well organized. Revelation 12:7 says, "There was war in heaven. Michael and his angels fought against the dragon, and the dragon and his angels fought back." Matthew 25:41 talks about "the eternal fire prepared for the devil and his angels."

The prince of Persia is obviously not a man, for no human could have resisted a messenger of God. He is supernatural, one of Satan's demon assistants. These creatures have special assignments on earth, and we see their imprint everywhere.

Satan and his demons are active in the world today. We see their destructive power far and wide, causing despair and destruction. The Prince of Darkness has been working to deceive and destroy from the beginning. The fact is, we are in a continual battle with Satan and his minions.

How does Satan accomplish his goals? He is not omnipresent. When we talk about Satan tempting us, it is probably not the Beast himself, but one of his demons he has sent to plague us. These evil angels come at every opportunity to tempt and draw us away from the things of God. This is what it means in Ephesians 6:12 when it says, "For we are not fighting against people made of flesh and blood, but against persons without bodies—the evil rulers of the unseen world, those mighty satanic beings and great evil princes of darkness who rule this world, and against huge numbers of wicked spirits in the spirit world" (TLB).

Evil is not abstract; it is not lurking out there somewhere like a cloud. Evil always has an intelligent, conscious source. There is no evil that does not originate in a personality. There is the evil that is within us, and there is the evil that is personally involved with Satan and his emissaries. He is organized, and his troops are everywhere.

When God's messenger was intercepted in the heavenlies, it was by a demon assigned to Persia. His orders from Satan were to do everything he could to keep God's plan in Persia from going forward.

Demons are assigned to the United States and are hovering over our elective process. They work overtime in the halls of government to abort the purpose of God and His plan.

Dr. Merrill Unger was a teacher of mine when I was a seminary student. In a classic book on demonology, he wrote:

> History, since the fall of man, has been an unbroken attestation to the ominous fact of evil powers in human rulers, whether it be a Pharaoh of Egypt, oppressing the people of God, or a Nebuchadnezzar, leading them into captivity, or a Nero, brutally torturing and massacring them. However, perhaps the most solemn demonstration of the utter barbarity and horrible cruelty and wickedness of men energized by demon power has, it seems, been reserved for the boasted civilization and enlightenment of the twentieth century.
>
> Hitler, the demon-energized and demon-directed scourge of Europe, has come and gone, leaving behind him only a trail of agonized suffering.[2]

When Hitler was getting ready to go on a major campaign, he often spent the majority of the night before, according to those around him, communing with the spirit world. He was in touch with his prince, and certainly evil angels were commissioned to direct the affairs of that wicked tyrant.

IF SATAN WAS JUDGED,
WHY IS HE WINNING?

"Since the children have flesh and blood, he too shared in their humanity so that by his death he might destroy him who holds the power of death—that is, the devil" (Heb. 2:14). Satan was judged at the cross, but for a defeated person he appears to be quite alive. He seems to have gained control of philosophy, religion, and politics; wormed into our homes; and destroyed nations. He has plenty of invading marauders doing his work.

Calvary's victory destroyed all the claims that Satan has upon us, but the enforcement of that victory is a different matter. Legally, all of his claims were canceled when the Lord died for us. But like any other legal victory, it must be enforced. Some day it will be enforced forever, when Satan is thrown into the pit of hell and his angels are consigned to perpetual torment. But he is loose today, even though judgment has been rendered.

If a man commits murder, he is breaking the law of the land. However, if there are no police to arrest him, courts to try him, or jails to contain him, there can be no enforcement of the law. Although Satan has been judged at the cross, that judgment has not yet been administered. One day that sentence will be carried out, and he will be banished forever from our presence.

There is a way to enforce Satan's sentence, and we are to be the enforcers. Our first weapon is the Word of God. Here is how we fight Satan and his demons:

Put on the full armor of God so that you can take your stand against the devil's schemes. For our struggle is not against flesh and blood, but against the rulers, against the authorities, against the powers of this dark world and against the spiritual forces of evil in the heavenly realms. Therefore put on the full armor of God, so that when the day of evil comes, you may be able to stand your ground, and after you have done everything, to stand. . . . Take the helmet of salvation and the sword of the Spirit, which is the word of God. And pray in the Spirit on all occasions with all kinds of prayers and requests. (Eph. 6:11–13, 17–18)

The next is prayer. The Bible has a key passage that teaches us the way to fight the battle:

The weapons we fight with are not the weapons of the world. On the contrary, they have divine power to demolish strongholds. We demolish arguments and every pretension that sets itself up against the knowledge of God, and we take captive every thought to make it obedient to Christ. (2 Cor. 10:4–5)

Why did the angel finally get to earth to speak with Daniel? I believe it was because Daniel never quit praying. The tool that enforces Satan's defeat is prayer. If we really believed that, then praying would be the main business of the church. But here is where Satan has defeated us. He keeps us so busy reading the latest bestsellers in the Christian bookstores, organizing all kinds of evangelistic strategies, counseling, and putting out the fires of opposition that we don't have time to pray. As we run around trying to get all the work done, we become so frustrated and fatigued that we wonder why we don't have the victory.

God has been teaching me that the only way we are going to have victory in a ministry, in a life, or in a church is to come to grips with the power that He has put in our hands through prayer.

If we are honest with ourselves, we would probably admit that we don't put a high priority on prayer. We give it a lick and a promise as often as we can. We pray before we go to bed (sometimes) and before we eat. Once in a while, when we get in real bad shape, we ask God to get us out of trouble. But when it comes to the fervent praying that makes a difference in our lives and the life of this earth, we scarcely give it lip service.

THE KEY TO MY SAFETY BOX

I have a safety deposit box at the bank. I'm not sure why, but we do keep some papers and certain valuables in there. I have a key (if I can find it), and when I go to the bank and want to get into the vault, there is a clerk who comes in and puts her key in the lock, too, so that the box is opened. Prayer is like that. There was a day when God put His key in the box and defeated Satan. The defeat will be implemented in our lives when we put the key of prayer in, turn it, and have the victory released to us.

We have not done so because we haven't asked. We are not victorious because we don't take what God has given us. We don't pray against Satan's strategy in our schools, in our homes, and in our countries. Many times we are praying to and praying for, but not praying against.

I was in the home of a good friend when he was having a devotional time with his family. I'll never forget it. He had his teenagers around the table, and he was praying for them. This is what he prayed, "Oh, God, keep my children from divorce." I thought, *This is strange, they aren't even married yet.* When we were alone I asked him about his prayer and he said, "I've been praying that ever since they became teenagers. I'm praying against every activity I can think of that Satan has in mind for those kids."

TARGET AREAS

I grew up in a town where there was a Christian college. Someone asked me why so many problems happen in Christian colleges. After all, you would think when Christians get together it would be utopia. I didn't understand this when I was younger, but I certainly do now. If we are afraid of Satan, the worst place for us to be is where there are a whole bunch of God's people. Satan and his helpers don't worry about the people "out there." He already has them. But when he gets his sights on a collection of future leaders, potential servants, ministers, and missionaries all gathered in one place, he doesn't have to send a whole lot of his angels down to do his job. He just blitzes us. It's a daily battle.

If we are going to survive for the grace and glory of God, we have to start praying. I'm not talking about the surface kind of praying, but the type of intensity that we see in this story of Daniel, where a man was so burdened he couldn't even eat. This is what being a prayer warrior means.

When Daniel prayed, he was also given the battle plan of Satan's number-one angel. We are living in an age when the armies of the end times are gathering their forces, and their strategy should not be a mystery to us.

18

BATTLEGROUND
OF DANIEL

The story is told of a professor at a liberal theological seminary who was teaching from the book of Daniel. His class consisted of young men and women, many of them future church leaders. At the beginning of his lecture he said, "Now I want you to understand that Daniel was written during the Maccabean period in the second century BC, not by the historic Daniel who lived in the sixth century BC. The facts were written, as all history is, after the events took place."

One young man raised his hand and asked, "How can that be, sir, when Christ said in Matthew 24:16 that it was written by Daniel?"

The professor paused a moment, looked the student in the eyes and said, "Young man, I know more about the book of Daniel than Jesus did."

Many students in that class are preaching in our churches today. This is what goes on in some seminaries across the country every day.

Remember the demons fought for twenty-one days, trying to keep God's special angelic messenger from delivering the prewritten story of history to His man, Daniel. Just as these prophecies were fought over in heaven before they got here, they will be fought over until the day Christ returns. The skeptics hate the Word of God, and they don't know what to do with detailed evidences like those we see in the eleventh chapter of this book.

John Walvoord, a great prophetic scholar, has written: "The issue is a clear-cut question of whether God is omniscient about the future. If He is, revelation may be just as detailed as God elects to make it; and detailed prophecy becomes no more difficult or incredible than broad predictions."[1]

Daniel had been praying for twenty-one days. He had assumed that after the seventy years of captivity, God would restore the people of Israel to their former state of glory. Instead, almost three years had passed, and while it was true that some people had returned to the city, nothing else seemed to be happening. Only the foundation of the temple had been built, and the Jews had begun to fight among themselves. Everything came to a stop. Daniel was frustrated and disappointed. *What are you doing, God?*

So finally the angel arrived on earth and began to tell him what God has in store for His people. This special envoy from God unfolded the exact history of what would happen to the nation of Israel for the next two to three hundred years. When we look at those prophecies today and see how accurate, detailed, and totally fulfilled they were, we must make a choice. Either we believe they are from God or we come up with another answer as some skeptics have done.

ANGEL MISSION

The angel had a mission. He was to show Daniel what God said would happen to the world, especially the nation of Israel, in the end times.

The first prophecy the angel brought to Daniel concerned the future of the Persian government. Daniel was living during the time of the Persians when King Cyrus had decreed the return of the Jews. The prophecy says, "Now then, I tell you the truth: Three more kings will appear in Persia, and then a fourth, who will be far richer than all the others" (Dan. 11:2).

This would be as if a well-known religious figure today had a visit from an angel, and he was told who the next several presidents of the United States would be. I wonder how many tabloids would print that story. But we are able to prove the validity of the angel's predictions because historically they happened exactly as he said.

The notable kings who came after Cyrus were, first, his son, Cambyses. After the heir apparent, the next king was Pseudo-Smerdis. This man with the weird name was an impostor. He gained access to the royal household because he looked like Cambyses' son, and he used his mistaken identity to become king. And so he was given the name Pseudo, or False-Smerdis.

The third king was Darius. The fourth king was Xerxes, but his other name was Ahasuerus. This was the king who is mentioned in the book of Esther and who commanded one of the largest armies the world had ever known. He wanted to defeat Greece but was totally routed and sent back home like a whimpering dog. After Ahasuerus checked out, another mighty king took center stage, and he is a person we have already met. His name is Alexander.

Then a mighty king will appear, who will rule with great power and do as he pleases. After he has appeared, his empire will be broken up and parceled out toward the four winds of heaven. It will not go to his descendants, nor will it have the power he exercised, because his empire will be uprooted and given to others. (Dan. 11:3–4)

That describes Alexander precisely. He was one of the most remarkable men who ever lived, and by the time he was thirty-three years old he had control of the world from Europe to India. But when he died, his kingdom was divided four ways. The Bible says that his kingdom would not go to his children.

Alexander had an illegitimate son and a legitimate son, the latter of whom was born after Alexander's death. His brother was mentally handicapped. Shortly after Alexander died, all three of these people were murdered.

The generals who fought over Alexander's kingdom eventually divided it four ways: Macedonia, Asia Minor, Egypt, and Syria. One of these generals ruled Egypt, which, if we know our geography, is south of Israel, and another ruled Syria, which is north. Out of Syria came the first king of the North, and from Egypt the king of the South. These two and their successors made life miserable for the Jews, who were caught in a vise between them.

TOUGH YEARS FOR THE JEWS

If a so-called modern-day prophet called a press conference and announced to the media, "Get ready for the scoop of the century. I am going to tell you exactly what will happen in the Middle East for the next two hundred years," I suppose everybody would leave except the reporters for the sensational tabloids.

In Daniel 11:5–35, we are told the detailed history of almost two hundred years of fighting between the king of the South and the king of the North. Some of these events sound like the worst soap-opera scenario, with daughters being bartered for favors, people being murdered because of jealousy, and a wife being put aside for a younger, prettier paramour.

History is not dull when we see how each event fits together in the jigsaw puzzle of prophecy. Not one piece is lost before the whole picture is seen. Here's one part of that picture:

> The king of the South will become strong, but one of his com-
> manders will become even stronger than he and will rule his own
> kingdom with great power. After some years, they will become
> allies. The daughter of the king of the South will go to the king
> of the North to make an alliance, but she will not retain her
> power, and he and his power will not last. In those days she will
> be handed over, together with her royal escort and her father and
> the one who supported her. (Dan. 11:5–6)

And what really happened? These two kings were constantly at each other's throats. In those days they had an interesting way of handling disagreements. If you were the king of the South and you weren't getting along with the king of the North, you'd take your daughter and offer her to the opposition. They used to marry their daughters off like a peace treaty.

So, the third king of Syria, who called himself Antiochus the God (quite an ego), decided to make a treaty with the king of the South and marry the daughter of the king of Egypt. One small detail: He was already married. No problem. He divorced his wife and married the daughter of the Egyptian king anyway. Now the wife of Antiochus didn't like that one bit, so she murdered his new wife and all of her attendants. Guess what the king did? He took his wife back. And as soon as they were remarried, she poisoned him.

Just as the verses above said, everybody involved lost: the

king's daughter, all of her attendants, and the king himself. The whole peace-treaty attempt was blown away.

However, the brother of the murdered Egyptian princess (v. 7, "One from her family line") started another war with the king of the North and won. Egypt and Syria were again at each other's throats, and the battle was fought on Israel's soil. Poor Israel was always caught in the middle, and it didn't seem possible that peace would ever come.

As the angel continued to tell Daniel these prophecies, our old friend must have been in a state of semi-shock. Generations of his people were doomed on the battlefields of warring nations.

In verses 10–19, we are told of another strong king who attempted to control and unite Syria and Egypt. History tells us that Antiochus the Great was king of the North and had a mighty army. He attacked Egypt with seventy-five thousand soldiers and stomped right through Israel to get there.

I'm certainly not a military strategist, but the seesaw battles that were carried on by these rulers seem almost ludicrous. The king of Syria retaliated with seventy-three thousand men, five thousand cavalry, and seventy-three elephants. (The elephants were used as battering rams.) Once more, Israel was in the middle. Can you imagine seventy-three elephants tromping all over the land?

Antiochus the Great was not to be outdone, and, just as the Scriptures said, "For the king of the North will muster another army, larger than the first; and after several years, he will advance with a huge army fully equipped. . . . The forces of the South will be powerless to resist; even their best troops will not have the strength to stand" (Dan. 11:13, 15).

Where does the conquering king go? "He will establish himself in the Beautiful Land and will have the power to destroy it" (Dan.

11:16). The poor Jews were getting trampled again, and they were not even involved in the conflict.

But Antiochus still wasn't happy with his victories. He was determined to unite Syria and Egypt, so what did he do? Of course, he decided to give the king of Egypt his daughter. His daughter was a very desirable woman. The king had hoped to put a spy in the palace, somebody on his side. The plan was thwarted, however, because the daughter fell in love with the Egyptian king and forgot all about Daddy.

Daddy was mad. When the plan with his daughter failed, he went on a rampage. The prophecy said, "Then he will turn his attention to the coastlands and will take many of them, but a commander will put an end to his insolence and will turn his insolence back upon him" (Dan. 11:18). Antiochus headed toward the coastlands, which was Greece, but the Roman armies that were on the ascension stood in his way, and he was routed. For the second time his plan was thwarted. History tells us that he went back to his own cities and tried to plunder the temple of Jupiter in his own land. Here was a guy who didn't care who was in his way as long as he was able to grab what he wanted. His own people were so angry at him that they murdered him. The Scriptures say that he "will stumble and fall, to be seen no more" (Dan. 11:19).

Antiochus was defeated and forgotten. The only reason we even mention him is because he fulfilled to the letter the message from the angel. He was replaced by a tax collector, who collected taxes to sustain the glory of the kingdom. He didn't last very long before someone we have heard of before came onto the scene. This fourth major king (after Ahasuerus, Alexander, and Antiochus the Great) was the infamous Antiochus Epiphanes. He was called "contemptible" and "vile." We described him before as the forerunner of the Antichrist.

Antiochus Epiphanes was one of the most wicked men who ever lived. He plotted his way into a place of power, and when he became king he began to devastate the Egyptians. He moved into the richest provinces and robbed them of all the valuables he could find. With the loot he bought the allegiance of the renegades he needed to perpetrate his crimes. He had an army of mercenaries to march against the king of the South.

Finally, the kings decided on a peace treaty. This must be a familiar ruse by this time for all of us who have watched the peace attempts. It says, "The two kings, with their hearts bent on evil, will sit at the same table and lie to each other" (Dan. 11:27).

Every peace treaty that has been made since the world began has been broken. This one was just like the rest.

The king of the North (Antiochus Epiphanes) went home for a time, but he was still determined to invade the South again. This time he had another foe, the "ships of the western coastlands." Some believe this is a reference to the Roman navy. At any rate, his plans were thwarted, and he vented his fury on the Jews. He unleashed a purge on the Jews that was so foul it is no wonder he has been called Antiochus the Madman.

However, if you want to read something that will thrill your soul, look at the books of the Maccabees in the Apocrypha. They are not inspired Scripture, but they describe the Maccabean revolt and the courageous men who fought against Antiochus Epiphanes. They hid out in the hills. Every time the madman tried to move, they would swarm in on him. Finally, the great stalwart patriot, Judas Maccabeus, led the revolt that brought this vile king's reign to an end.

An entire era of history was covered in this portion of Daniel. It is another place where the book of Daniel is especially fitted to be a battleground between faith and unbelief.

CHOOSE SIDES

I remember a lesson that I had years ago in Sunday school. Our teachers placed two chairs in front of the class, and on one they had a sign that read, "Naturalist." On the other was a sign that read, "Supernaturalist." They said, "Kids, someday you are going to have to decide which of these two chairs you are sitting in. If you sit in the naturalist chair, you are going to want to figure everything out rationally and will only take those things which you have been able to observe through what we call the scientific process. Somewhere along the way you may decide you want to get out of that chair and sit in the chair of the supernaturalist. If you do, you are in good stead with Genesis 1:1, which says, 'In the beginning God . . . .' That's where it all starts."

If we believe that God is able to create the world, then it seems to me if He wanted to accurately prophesy a little section of history to give us insight into His prophetic mind, then He certainly is capable of doing that.

I've had people say to me, "Pastor Jeremiah, I've got to be honest with you. I don't believe all this stuff."

The story is told about a man out on Long Island who for years dreamed of owning a very special barometer. He finally saw one in a mail-order catalog and ordered it. When he unpacked the instrument, he was dismayed that the needle on his brand new barometer was set and seemed to be stuck pointing to the section marked "HURRICANE." He took it out of the box and shook it for all it was worth, but he couldn't get it to work right. He wrote a scorching letter to the catalog house and mailed his protest while he was on his way to the office in New York the next morning.

That evening when he got back to Long Island, he found that

not only was the barometer missing, but so was his house. The barometer had been right. There had been a hurricane.

We have seen the accurate fulfillment of prophecies through Daniel. Now we move up to the stage in history where the prophecies are for a time yet in the future.

Whether we believe them or not, what God has said *will* come to pass. Are you ready?

CHAPTER 19

A TIME YET TO COME

When Daniel prayed as the seventy years of captivity were almost over, he assumed the nation of Israel was immediately going to be restored to its place of glory. But God sent his angel to him with a message about Israel's future that wasn't encouraging.

All the kings of the North and the South, the despots and conquerors who trampled over the land of Palestine for years, literally fulfilled the prophecy that said that the land of Israel would be trodden down by the Gentiles until the time of the end (Luke 21:24).

In the end times there is going to be another influence that comes upon that land from the Roman dominion. This is preparation for the Armageddon countdown, and it will take place just as surely as all of the previous prophecies have been fulfilled.

The angel of prophecy takes Daniel from about two hundred years in the future to more than two thousand years ahead. Now we see another king. This one makes Antiochus Epiphanes look like a boy scout.

> The king will do as he pleases. He will exalt and magnify himself above every god and will say unheard-of things against the

God of gods. He will be successful until the time of wrath is completed, for what has been determined must take place. (Dan. 11:36)

This king will do as he pleases, for he will rule the world for a time and bring about more persecutions, murders, hatred, and turmoil than has ever been seen. He is the Antichrist.

PREPARATION FOR ARMAGEDDON

The world is no stranger to war. Since the beginning of our country, we have experienced a major war about every twenty-five years, starting with the War of Independence in 1776, the War of 1812, the Civil War, the Spanish-American War, World Wars I and II, the Korean War, the Vietnam War, and the ongoing war against terror. Scarcely a generation has passed in which this so-called Christian nation has not sent its young people to war.

The Bible says the disaster that will draw the curtain on modern civilization is definitely a predicted war called Armageddon. This will not be just a war, but a battle fought on different fronts. Preparation for that battle is now taking place.

The Bible teaches us that the only thing that remains before the Antichrist begins his rule is the disappearance of all true believers in Jesus Christ, which is called the Rapture of the church. When the Holy Spirit is restrained, in the sense that He is the controlling influence on the evil in this world, then all hell is going to break loose.

Revelation 12:13 tells us that when Satan is cast out of heaven and onto the earth in the middle of the Tribulation, he will begin immediately to persecute the woman who brought forth the male child, which I believe is the nation of Israel. His purpose is to destroy the Jews. Cooperating with Satan is the Antichrist, who is the head of the reestablished Roman Empire, and the false prophet, the head of the great religious system. Here is the unholy trinity. We could be only a short time away from this great holocaust.

PLACE OF ARMAGEDDON

Armageddon is a reference to the mountain of Megiddo, a geographical location in northern Israel. It is an extended plain that reaches from the Mediterranean Sea to the northern part of the land of Israel. Napoleon said that perhaps no other location in the world presents such a natural arena where the armies of the world might gather together in conflict.[1] Napoleon was no prophet, but he called that one right!

The battle of Armageddon is not localized on the plain of Megiddo, but spreads out in different places throughout the land of Israel. The whole land will be involved in the bloody clash. The Scripture says that blood will flow to the height of a horse's bridle and will extend from the northern end of Israel down to the southern tip. This is not just a single battle that will start in a moment and be over, but a campaign that will involve many battles and skirmishes at the end time.

THE PURPOSE OF ARMAGEDDON

It is revolting to think of such carnage, and we cannot read those words without wondering what kind of God would allow such a bloodbath to take place in His world. Why is it that such a terrible world war will take place?

We have seen that Daniel's heart was broken because those who returned to Jerusalem to rebuild the temple were only back there a short time before they fell into the same kind of sin that caused them to be exiled in the first place. The Jews were a stubborn and rebellious people as it relates to their God. God promised Daniel that He was not finished judging them yet. We call the Tribulation the "Time of Jacob's Trouble." It is the time of the punishment of the Jewish people for their rebellion.

Another reason for the great Armageddon campaign is so that the nations can be judged for their persecution of Israel. God has promised the Jewish people that those who persecute them would be persecuted and those who bless them would be blessed. God is faithful to His promise. Those nations that have persecuted the Jews are finally gathered together in the battle of Armageddon, and God's wrath is let loose upon them.

It seems rather strange that God is judging the Jews, and then He turns around and punishes others who deal harshly with them. It's only a reminder that judgment belongs to the Lord and to nobody else. He is going to deal harshly with those who do not treat His people fairly.

This will be a time when God will judge all the nations for their sinfulness. When I look out at this world and see the evil that runs rampant, not only in our culture but in the cultures of the other nations, I wonder how long God can go on before He rains judgment down upon the world.

Some say, "But it has always been this way." No, it hasn't! I don't think there has been a time in the history of our country when immorality has been so unrestrained as it is today.

Daniel's message is a reminder to us that though God may delay His judgment, He will not forget it. One of these days, He will have had enough, and we will have crossed over that line from which there can be no repentance.

Revelation 16:9 says: "They were seared by the intense heat and they cursed the name of God, who had control over these plagues, but they refused to repent and glorify him."

Even with the awfulness of the judgment that is associated with Armageddon, the Scripture says that the wicked men who are punished by God will continue to curse God to His face and not repent. The campaign of Armageddon is sort of a visual aid of the wrath of God at work upon those who have rejected Him.

PARTICIPANTS IN THE BATTLE

First, there will be a ten-nation confederacy under the leadership of the Antichrist. We have already studied that the Antichrist will be a vital force to bring together all the European powers into a coalition of governments.

Daniel was given another description of this infamous character:

> He will show no regard for the gods of his fathers or for the one desired by women, nor will he regard any god, but will exalt himself above them all. Instead of them, he will honor a god of fortresses; a god unknown to his fathers he will honor with gold and silver, with precious stones and costly gifts. He will attack the mightiest fortresses with the help of a foreign god and will greatly honor those who acknowledge him. He will make them rulers over many people and will distribute the land at a price. (Dan. 11:37–39)

When the Antichrist heads up the nations of the revived Roman Empire, many people wonder where America will be in all of this. Dr. Dwight Pentecost, a noted prophetic scholar, said this:

> Now what is our origin, politically, socially, economically, and linguistically? We have come from the nations that originally belonged to the Roman empire. Our customs and laws have all

come from that European background, from nations that emerged out of the Roman empire. Daniel speaks of those nations as the ten horns and the ten toes that will be brought together under the power and the authority of the beast. Even though we are not one of the ten by virtue of the fact that we did not emerge directly out of the old Roman empire, we may be one of the ten by virtue of our heritage. The United States may well cast her lot with Europe and come into this confederation of nations, and become part of that confederacy that will be drawn into conflict, and will be judged by the Lord at his second coming. It is interesting to note that this confederation of the former Roman empire nations includes almost all of the nominal Christian nations.[2]

Pentecost wrote these words many years before American leaders began to talk about a global economy and the new world order.

The second player involved in the end-times battles is the king of the North, which includes the major powers north of Israel: Syria, Turkey, and, of course, the vast area of Russia.

The third player in this great cast are the kings of the East, from the area beyond the Euphrates. This includes China, Japan, and other countries in Asia.

Then we have the Lord and His armies. We will see how they fit into this picture.

Finally, the last combatant is the nation of Israel. One of the most interesting things about the battle of Armageddon is that the nation of Israel is again passive. This country has been fought against and overrun by all the other nations, but in the final campaign they are inactive. This seems strange in light of what we know about Israel today and its amazing technological and military might. At the time of the end Israel is almost a bystander while the nation is being trampled over for the last time.

SEQUENCE OF EVENTS

The first and most important event is the covenant that will be made between the Antichrist and Israel. According to Daniel 9:27, the prince that shall come makes a covenant with the nation of Israel. He is going to go to the Jewish people at the beginning of the Tribulation period and promise them that their sacrifices, temple worship, and their opportunity to get back into Judaism as they once knew in the glory days can be theirs once again. The Jews will swallow it completely. This prince, who is the head of the European confederation, will also make a treaty between all the European nations and Israel, guaranteeing protection. The result will be that the Jews will become lethargic about their own defense and will put their guns down as they are lulled into a spirit of protection. Just as they are about to go to sleep in their peace, something is going to happen.

Why would the Jews let down their defenses? Because the Antichrist will assure them that everything is great; he is taking care of them personally! While the Antichrist and his coalition are supposedly protecting Israel, the king of the North (Russia and its allies) and the king of the South (the Northern African powers) will decide to come after the Antichrist and his coalition government.

> At the time of the end the king of the South will engage him in battle, and the king of the North will storm out against him with chariots and cavalry and a great fleet of ships. (Dan. 11:40)

Now we are about to see the next player in this final drama. "But reports from the east and the north will alarm him" (Dan. 11:44). The reports from the east are those armies that Revelation tells us will come in with two hundred million soldiers marching across the dried-up riverbed of the Euphrates.

Now the stage is set. Just at the moment when Israel and Jerusalem are about to be attacked and their annihilation seems certain, the battle of Armageddon takes place. As I write about this, I fairly want to shout!

Here is how it ends:

> I saw heaven standing open and there before me was a white horse, whose rider is called Faithful and True. With justice he judges and makes war. His eyes are like blazing fire, and on his head are many crowns. He has a name written on him that no one knows but he himself. He is dressed in a robe dipped in blood, and his name is the Word of God. The armies of heaven were following him, riding on white horses and dressed in fine linen, white and clean. Out of his mouth comes a sharp sword with which to strike down the nations. "He will rule them with an iron scepter." He treads the winepress of the fury of the wrath of God Almighty. On his robe and on his thigh he has this name written: KING OF KINGS AND LORD OF LORDS. (Rev. 19:11–16)

When the nations that are gathered together against Jerusalem see the Lord's armies in heaven coming after them, they will forget about the fact that they are at war with each other. They will all get together and decide they are going to fight against the Lord.

All the armies with their military leaders and advanced technology won't have a chance. After the Antichrist is captured, and the false prophet, too, the two of them will be thrown alive into the lake of fire.

> The rest of them were killed with the sword that came out of the mouth of the rider on the horse, and all the birds gorged themselves on their flesh. (Rev. 19:21)

The Bible says that immediately upon the conquest, the nations will be established as His kingdom upon this earth.

As we read the news today, we can see that God is getting everything in place to begin the final events. What is our response? We need to ask God to build within us a holy urgency for the cause of Jesus Christ, based upon the fact that He is coming soon!

20

THE END TIMES

When I was growing up, we used to watch *Alfred Hitchcock Presents* on black-and-white television. His complex mystery plots would sometimes leave me in such suspense that I would storm around the house muttering, "It's not fair to leave someone hanging up in space like that, not knowing what's going on." (I only use that phrase in the figurative sense.)

When we come to the end of the book of Daniel, there's a deep desire to find out how all of this is going to end. Daniel has been told about some very difficult days that are coming for his people and he knows that a terrible battle will take place in the country he loves. The end of his vision of the future, which began in chapter 10 of Daniel and was conveyed to him by the messenger angel, has its climax in the Tribulation and the resurrection that follows.

The eleventh chapter of Daniel dealt primarily with the political and religious aspects of the time of the end. The twelfth and final chapter relates this same period to the people of Israel—what will happen to them and what that means to us.

PAIN SO GREAT

This is what we read in Daniel 12:1: "At that time Michael, the great prince who protects your people, will arise. There will be a time of distress such as has not happened from the beginning of nations until then."

Before Daniel was captive in Babylon, another great prophet lived in Jerusalem. Here is what God spoke through him about that time:

> "The days are coming," declares the LORD, "when I will bring my people Israel and Judah back from captivity and restore them to the land I gave their forefathers to possess," says the LORD.
>
> These are the words the LORD spoke concerning Israel and Judah: "This is what the LORD says:
>
> "'Cries of fear are heard—
> terror, not peace.
> Ask and see:
> Can a man bear children?
> Then why do I see every strong man
> with his hands on his stomach like a woman in labor,
> every face turned deathly pale?
> How awful that day will be!
> None will be like it.
> It will be a time of trouble for Jacob,
> but he will be saved out of it.'" (Jer. 30:3–7)

The time of Jacob's trouble is going to be like a whole nation going through the unbelievable agony that only a woman who has given birth to a child can understand. I don't think there is anything more excruciating than the pain a woman goes through when she's having a baby. I know some men have taken all the classes and even gone into the delivery room and been a part of that beautiful experience. I have not done it. In fact, when our last child was born, as my wife was being taken into the delivery room, the doctor asked the nurse, "Is she ready?" The nurse answered, "No, but I don't think her husband can last much longer." I cannot stand to see someone I love in pain, and I believe that if God didn't miraculously erase the pain of childbirth from a woman's mind, I doubt if anyone would ever have more than one child.

In the twenty-fourth chapter of Matthew, Jesus describes the Tribulation as a time of trouble such as has not been known from the beginning of the world, nor ever shall be until that time.

In Revelation 6–19 the apostle John talks about war, famine, 25 percent of the world being killed, one-third of the earth and the sea destroyed, fresh water being polluted, the release of hell's demons to overrun the earth, and more ghastly occurrences.

The Tribulation is not just more trouble than we have now. The Bible is too graphic to allow for that rationale.

SUPERANGEL RETURNS

When we see conflict, Michael always seems to be involved. In the New Testament book of Jude, Michael had personal combat with the devil himself. Now here he is involved in the conflict for Israel. The Bible says he will protect the people.

Although Daniel didn't know the details, he was given a glimpse of what John wrote more than six hundred years later in the twelfth chapter of Revelation. Satan hates Israel because it is from that nation that the Redeemer was brought into the world. He tried to keep the Lord Jesus from being born, and he did everything in his own power to destroy Him. In the Tribulation period, Satan will pour out his wrath upon the Jewish nation. People who are anti-Semitic are keeping bad company with the original anti-Semite, Satan himself. The Tribulation period is Satan's final attempt to wipe Israel off the face of the earth.

While the Tribulation is going on down here, Michael and the dragon (Satan and his horde of evil angels) are having a war in the heavenlies. Once more, the prince of Israel is protecting "your people."

WHO ARE "YOUR PEOPLE"?

"But at that time your people—everyone whose name is found written in the book—will be delivered" (Dan. 12:1).

We know that the period of time is the Tribulation, and that the prince of Israel is Michael, who is doing everything he can to hold up the cause of the children of Israel. There are actually three categories of people who are the children of Israel. First, there are the rescued people, then the resurrected people, and finally the rewarded people. Every Jew and Gentile in the world should be alerted to the destiny of God's chosen people.

The Bible says that out of the Tribulation period some of the Jews are going to be rescued. There will be hundreds of thousands of Jews who will be killed during that time, but some of them will be saved. They will be the people who will establish the kingdom in the Millennium.

The prophet Jeremiah said:

> "I am with you and will save you,"
> declares the LORD.

"Though I completely destroy all the nations
among which I scatter you,
I will not completely destroy you.
I will discipline you but only with justice;
I will not let you go entirely unpunished." (Jer. 30:11; see also
 Ezek. 20:33–38)

Through the Tribulation period, the unbelieving Jews—those who do not honor God—are going to be destroyed, but a certain number of them will be left. The astonishing thing (although we shouldn't be surprised by the detail of prophecy by this time) is that the Bible tells us exactly how many Jews are going to make it through the Tribulation, untouched by God's judgment. This is what the prophet Zechariah said:

"In the whole land," declares the LORD,
"two-thirds will be struck down and perish;
yet one-third will be left in it.
This third I will bring into the fire;
I will refine them like silver
and test them like gold.
They will call on my name
and I will answer them;
I will say, 'They are my people,'
and they will say, 'The LORD is our God.'" (Zech. 13:8–9)

I think one of the hardest verses in the Bible to understand is the one that says in the end times, "all Israel will be saved" (Rom. 11:26). That has really puzzled me because God doesn't work that way. He doesn't save nations; He saves individuals. But now it is clear to me, because what God tells us is that by a particular time in the Tribulation, the only Jews who are left will be those who have believed in the Messiah. So *all* Israel shall be saved.

The purpose of the Tribulation period, as far as the Jews are concerned, is to purge out that rebellious part of the Jewish nation and do away with apostate Judaism. That which is left at the end of that period is the righteous nation of Israel that will ultimately go into the Millennium with Jesus Christ as King.

One-third of the Jews are going to be rescued.

The second category of people are those who are resurrected: "Multitudes who sleep in the dust of the earth will awake: some to everlasting life, others to shame and everlasting contempt" (Dan. 12:2).

There's an old spiritual tune that talks about "That great gettin' up mornin'," which is meant to describe everybody getting up out of their graves. This is a great song, but it isn't biblical, because the Bible doesn't teach one general resurrection.

The first resurrection the Bible teaches is Christ's resurrection. When He was resurrected, He was the guarantee that someday we shall be resurrected (1 Cor. 15:12–20). If we die before the Second Coming of Jesus Christ, the Bible says that someday we shall be resurrected: "For the Lord himself will come down from heaven, with a loud command, with the voice of the archangel and with the trumpet call of God, and the dead in Christ will rise first. After that, we who are still alive and are left will be caught up together with them in the clouds to meet the Lord in the air. And so we will be with the Lord forever" (1 Thess. 4:16–17).

The third resurrection of God's saved people comes at the end of the Tribulation period (Rev. 21:4). At that resurrection, all of the Old Testament saints are resurrected, as well as all of those who died during the Tribulation period. So we have the resurrection of the saved in three installments: Christ, the church, and the Old

Testament saints with those who died in the Tribulation. This is the resurrection of the just.

The second part of the resurrection is of the unjust. In Daniel 12, the first resurrection is "some to everlasting life," but the second part is "others to shame and everlasting contempt."

At the end of the Millennium all of the unsaved dead are resurrected and immediately stand before the Great White Throne Judgment (Rev. 20:5–6). Daniel didn't see this as we see it, because from the close of the first resurrection until the second resurrection, there will be a thousand years. When the prophets saw into the future, they didn't see spans of time that would occur between one prophecy and the next. The Bible is very clear that by the time God is finished resurrecting, nobody will be left in the grave.

When the angel tells Daniel about "your people," he describes those who are rescued, those who are resurrected, and the last group, the rewarded: "Those who are wise will shine like the brightness of the heavens, and those who lead many to righteousness, like the stars for ever and ever" (Daniel 12:3).

In the midst of all the difficult times, the horror of the Tribulation, God has some special things that He has reserved for those who serve Him. He says they are going to become stars in His galaxy!

I believe the word *wise* refers to being a teacher. God says that during that time of awful trouble on the Jewish nation, He is going to raise up some who will be teachers of righteousness. Can you imagine what it will cost a person to stand up in the Tribulation period with a Bible in hand and declare the righteousness of God? Those people know that when they teach the truth of God, their heads could roll at any moment. There is a special place in God's kingdom for those who accurately teach God's holy Book.

I believe the second group of people will be those who run around during the Tribulation evangelizing, bringing others into a saving knowledge of Christ. We talk about how hard it is today to share our faith. Why is it hard? Because we are cowards. We don't like rejection. Can you imagine what it will be like in that day to witness, with the penalty of death on the head of the person who doesn't obey the Antichrist? Those special people will be stars.

Living in Southern California as I do, there is a lot of emphasis on celebrities. But you know what? Ten years from now nobody will think about them. They may be a pleasant or unpleasant memory, but the public will shift its allegiance to the newest personality who comes along.

God's program is different. One of my favorite pastors was W. A. Criswell. He had a way of putting things in perspective. He wrote: "Who are God's great? Who are these who will shine forever and ever? The answer is not they whom the world magnifies, exalts and applauds. Rather, it is God's humblest person who points a soul to Jesus. I think that is one of the most significant things that God reveals to us in His Word. How fleeting, how transitory, is the nobility of the world. It passes away like a mist."[1]

Isn't it thrilling that in the midst of this dark hour for Israel, when everything is bleak and hope is lost, God says that there are going to be some who are teachers of righteousness and some who are evangelists? Those who are faithful in that terrible time are going to be placed in the great galaxy of stars, never to burn out.

God will never allow His people to go unrewarded.

CLOSE THE BOOK, DANIEL

At the very beginning of this book, we said Daniel teaches us that God is in control. He is on the throne. Nothing happens accidentally before God. Kingdoms may rise and fall, but the kingdom of God is everlasting.

I believe we need a prophetic perspective on life. If we do not have this perspective, we will get caught up in trying to do the things that God says He alone can do, trying to get the kingdoms of this world under our control and manipulate them our way.

Daniel had a clear understanding of the sovereignty of God through the empires of Babylon, Medo-Persia, Greece, and Rome which he foretold and the time when God will bring down the curtain on the program of Satan.

In the last word from Daniel, he confessed twice that there was a whole lot that God had been teaching him which he didn't understand.

God told Daniel, "But you, Daniel, close up and seal the words of the scroll until the time of the end. Many will go here and there to increase knowledge" (Dan. 12:4). God was saying several things. "Daniel, there is no more information coming. That's the last word. Put a period at the end of the book." Also, "Make sure this book is preserved, because it is going to come into great meaning at a time in the future."

There is a time yet to come when an understanding of the book of Daniel will be even greater than it is now. I believe that will be in the time of the end when many are going to be running back and forth, trying to figure out what is happening in their world. Ultimately, they are going to discover answers to their questions in this book we have been studying.

I am convinced that in the Tribulation the book of Daniel will be the most important reading matter for many people. Imagine some innocent person who doesn't know a great deal about the Word of God, cast into the midst of hell on earth. He says, "Can somebody tell me what's going on?" Someone says, "Let me give you this book. It's the writing of an old sage by the name of Daniel."

I believe there will be some classes on Daniel in the Tribulation like you've never heard in your life. They are going to be able to understand better than we do, because while they are reading it, the events are going to be lived out right in front of them.

The prophetic seal was put on Daniel.

Daniel was still by the bank of the Tigris, receiving his last vision from the angel, when he looked up and saw two angels, one on each side of the river. He must have blinked his eyes and looked again, because hovering over the river was a man clothed in linen. The angels began to ask questions that Daniel probably wanted to ask. One said, "How long will it be before these astonishing things are fulfilled?" (Dan. 12:6).

I think the angels were saying, "How long are we going to have to go on with this? We would like to be discharged; we're getting tired of fighting with the demons."

The angel answered, "It will be for a time, times and half a time. When the power of the holy people has been finally broken, all these things will be completed" (Dan. 12:7).

The angel said that during the Tribulation the people of Israel will have their power shattered. The rebellious, disobedient Jews who refuse to embrace the Lord Jesus as their Messiah are going to be destroyed, but one-third of them will be saved.

Daniel, this great prophet, didn't understand. And the angel answered him in a most astounding way.

He replied, "Go your way, Daniel, because the words are closed up and sealed until the time of the end. Many will be purified, made spotless and refined, but the wicked will continue to be wicked. None of the wicked will understand, but those who are wise will understand." (Daniel 12:9–10)

The angel told Daniel that He was not going to give him any more information. He said, "Look, Daniel, there's no time for idle preoccupation in the prophetic realm." How that word is needed today! There are many who are making megabucks in the prophetic world, saying that the Rapture will happen at a certain time. The truth is, we don't know. Many people are led astray by all the craziness of date setting. We don't want to get caught in that trap.

It seems to me that Daniel 12:10 is the best commentary on our society that I have read in a long time. "Many will be purified, made spotless and refined." People are coming to Christ all over the world. Some people even believe this is the beginning of a great, wide-sweeping revival. "But the wicked will continue to be wicked. None of the wicked will understand, but those who are wise will understand" (Dan. 12:10). There has never been a time when there has been more wickedness than there is now. The wicked may even hear the gospel, but they don't have a clue as to what it means to them.

TROUBLE WITH NUMBERS

The Lord was still answering Daniel's question about the outcome of all this. He finished with these mystifying numbers:

> From the time that the daily sacrifice is abolished and the abomination that causes desolation is set up, there will be 1,290 days. Blessed is the one who waits for and reaches the end of the 1,335 days. (Daniel 12:11)

We know that in the middle of the Tribulation period, the abomination of desolation is set up. Previously we saw a lot of numbers in this book, and we've tried to make them all fit together. But the 1,290 days does not match the 1,260 days we've seen before. I'm asking, "Lord, where did that other month come from?" Then we are told that the end will come after 1,335 days.

That's 45 days' difference. I have some sanctified guesses, but I do not believe it's wise scholarship to theorize. It's not hard for me to understand why Daniel said, "I heard, but I did not understand" (Dan. 12:8).

God has a plan, and when He is ready to reveal it, He will!

GET INVOLVED!

God told Daniel three things when He finished this prophecy. These are what He wants to say to us today. "As for you, go your way till the end. You will rest, and then at the end of the days you will rise to receive your allotted inheritance" (Daniel 12:13).

Daniel was in his nineties. He was about ready to check out. God had given him all this wonderful truth, and now it was over. He said, "Go back to what you were supposed to be doing. Get involved. Take care of your responsibilities."

When we study prophecy, we get so enamored with the mystery of it all that we neglect to focus on the reason for our study. God wants us to get so stirred up that we share this knowledge with others, get involved in the lives of others, and pass on these timeless truths.

Then God told Daniel, "Go your way now, my friend, you deserve to rest. But you are going to be resurrected. One day you are going to arise!"

What a great promise. Daniel's long, strange, wonderful journey was about to end. No more would he be the target for cruel, jealous office seekers. He had seen the last of the den of hungry lions. His righteous soul would cease to be plagued by the sins of either Jew or Gentile. Daniel would rest and await the resurrection morning, when he will be richly rewarded by his wonderful Redeemer and King.

When our work is done, may we hear the wonderful words of our Lord, "Go and rest."

Last, there is the promise of reward. God told Daniel he would receive an inheritance at the end of his days.

We know that Daniel spent most of his life away from his homeland in a foreign culture. He died as an exile, but someday, God said, he would be a part of the redistribution of the land in the kingdom age. Daniel had a special reservation to be with the Lord.

At the end of Daniel's journey, God had another wonderful promise for Daniel. He has told us that we may have a special reservation too.

We are living in the time of the end. Have we learned from the experience of this man who lived more than twenty-five hundred years ago?

After our journey with Daniel, we should be able to read the handwriting on the wall, just as he did in those centuries past.

NOTES

CHAPTER 1: A PROPHET FOR OUR TIME

1. Joan Brown, *Corrie—The Lives She's Touched* (Old Tappan, NJ: Fleming H. Revell, 1979), 14.

CHAPTER 2: HISTORY IN A CAPSULE

1. Allan Bloom, *The Closing of the American Mind* (New York, NY: Simon & Schuster, 1987), 18–19.

CHAPTER 3: TRAINING OF A CHAMPION

1. Horatio Richmond Palmer, "Have Courage to Say No!" 1887.

CHAPTER 4: NIGHT DREAMS AND DAY VISIONS

1. Graham Scroggie, cited by Geoffrey King, Daniel, *A Detailed Explanation of the Book* (London: Henry E. Walker, 1966), 31.
2. Ruth Bell Graham, *Sitting by My Laughing Fire* (Waco, TX: Word, 1977), 32.
3. Edward Gibbon, *The Decline and Fall of the Roman Empire*, cited by Joseph A. Seiss, *Voices from Babylon* (Philadelphia, PA: Castle Press, 1879).
4. Alexander Fraser Tytler, *Decline and Fall of the Athenian Republic*, (1748–1813), n.p., n.d.
5. Franklin Belden, "Look for the Way-Marks," *Traditionalmusic. co.uk*, 1886.

CHAPTER 5: WHEN CHRIST RULES THE WORLD

1. Charles Wesley, "Lo, He Comes with Clouds Descending," *The Celebration Hymnal* (Word Music/Integrity, 1977).

CHAPTER 6: FIERY FAITH

1. *The Nineteenth Century and After,* Volume 121 (New York, NY: Leonard Scott Publishing Company, 1937), 154.
2. Ibid.
3. John Calvin, edited by Anthony Uyl, *Harmony of the Law—Volume II* (Woodstock, Ontario: Devoted Publishing, 2018), 107.
4. G. A. Studdert Kennedy, *The Hardest Part* (Charleston, SC: Bibliolife, 2009) 110–111.
5. Quoted in W. A. Criswell, "For God Forever," W. A. Criswell Sermon Library, June 7, 1970, https://www.wacriswell.com /sermons/1970/for-god-forever/.

CHAPTER 7: THE GOSPEL ACCORDING TO NEBUCHADNEZZAR

1. Billy Graham, *Peace with God: The Secret of Happiness* (Nashville, TN: Thomas Nelson, 2009) 26.

CHAPTER 8: YOUR NUMBER IS UP

1. Joseph A. Seiss, *Voices from Babylon* (Philadelphia, PA: Castle Press, 1879), 59.
2. Joseph Parker, *Preaching Through the Bible* (Grand Rapids, MI: Baker Books, 1960), 63–64.
3. Knowles Shaw, "The Handwriting on the Wall," 1877.

CHAPTER 9: POLITICAL INTRIGUE

1. Alexander McClaren, *Expositions of Holy Scripture* (London: Hodder & Stoughton, 1908).
2. Charles H. Spurgeon, "Clean Inside and Out," July 21, 2018, dailyintheword.org/rooted/clean-inside-and-out.
3. Sam Foss, "Cyrus Brown's Prayer," *Sourcebook of Poetry*, compiled

by Al Bryant (Grand Rapids, MI: Zondervan Publishing Co., 1963), 72–74.

CHAPTER 10: THE GREAT RESCUE

1. William Shakespeare, "The Tragedy of Julius Caesar," Scene 1: Rome.
2. Annie Johnson Flint as quoted in J. Oswald Sanders, *Robust in Faith: Men from God's School* (Chicago, IL: Moody Press, 1965), 169.
3. John Bunyan, *Grace Abounding to the Chief of Sinners* (Hertfordshire: Evangelical Press, 1978), 123.

CHAPTER 11: GOD'S INCREDIBLE PLAN FOR THE NATIONS

1. John F. Walvoord, "Chapter 7: Daniel's Vision of Future World History," accessed October 8, 2018, https://walvoord.com/article/248#P925_393794.

CHAPTER 14: DOWN ON OUR KNEES

1. E. M. Blaiklock, *The Positive Power of Prayer* (Glendale, CA: Regal, 1974), 43.
2. Mark Fackler, "The World Has Yet to See . . . ," *Christian History*, accessed October 9, 2018, https://www.christianitytoday.com/history/issues/issue-25/world-has-yet-to-see.html.

CHAPTER 15: UNLOCKING THE PROPHETIC WORD

1. "Our Story," *Chosen People Ministries*, accessed October 9, 2018, https://www.chosenpeople.com/site/our-mission-statement/our-story/.
2. Isaac Newton, *Observations upon the Prophecies of Daniel and the Apocalypse of St. John* (London: J. Darby and T. Browne, 1733).

CHAPTER 17: DEMON POWER

1. Adapted from Donald Campbell, *Daniel: God's Man in a Secular Society* (Grand Rapids, MI: Discovery House, 1988), 153.

2. Merrill F. Unger, *Biblical Demonology: A Study of the Spiritual Forces Behind the Present World Unrest* (Wheaton, IL: Van Kampen Press, Inc., 1952), 197.

CHAPTER 18: BATTLEGROUND OF DANIEL

1. John F. Walvoord, *Daniel: The Key to Prophetic Revelation* (Chicago, IL: The Moody Bible Institute of Chicago, 1971), 253.

CHAPTER 19: A TIME YET TO COME

1. Vernon J. McGee, *Through the Bible, vol. 3* (Nashville, TN: Thomas Nelson, Inc., 1982), 513.

2. Dwight Pentecost, *Will Man Survive?* (Chicago, IL: Moody Press, 1971), 130–131.

CHAPTER 20: THE END TIMES

1. W. A. Criswell, *Expository Sermons on the Book of Daniel* (Grand Rapids, MI.: Zondervan Publishing Co., 1972), 137.

RESOURCES

Anderson, Robert. *The Coming Prince*. Grand Rapids, Mich.: Kregel, 1954.

Bainton, Roland H. *Here I Stand*. New York: New American Library, 1950.

Blair, J. Allen. *Living Courageously*. Neptune, N.J.: Loizeux Brothers, 1971.

Bloom, Allan. *The Closing of the American Mind*. New York: Simon & Schuster, 1987.

Brown, Joan. *Corrie—The Lives She's Touched*. Old Tappan, N.J.: Fleming H. Revell, 1979.

Criswell, W. A. *Expository Sermons on the Book of Daniel*. Grand Rapids, Mich.: Zondervan Publishing Co., 1972.

Flint, Annie Johnson. "Sometimes." In *Treasury of 400 Quotable Poems*, compiled by Croft M. Pentz. Grand Rapids, Mich.: Zondervan Publishing Co., 1963.

Foss, Sam. "Cyrus Brown's Prayer." In *Sourcebook of Poetry*, compiled by Al Bryant. Grand Rapids, Mich.: Zondervan Publishing Co., 1963.

Foxe, John. *Foxe's Book of Martyrs*. Edited by Wm. Byrur Forbust. Philadelphia: John C. Winston Co., 1926.

Gibbon, Edward. *The Decline and Fall of the Roman Empire*, cited by Joseph A. Seiss, *Voices from Babylon*. Philadelphia: Castle Press, 1879.

Graham, Ruth Bell. *Sitting by My Laughing Fire*. Waco, Tex.: Word, 1977.

Heslop, W. G. *Diamonds from Daniel*. Grand Rapids, Mich.: Kregel Publications, 1976.

Jeremiah, David. *Escape the Coming Night*. Dallas: Word Publishing, 1990.

Jerome. *Commentary on Daniel*. Translated by Gleason L. Archer, Jr. Grand Rapids, Mich.: Baker Books, 1959.

King, Geoffrey. *Daniel, A Detailed Explanation of the Book*. London: Henry Walter, 1966.

McClaren, Alexander. *Expositions of Holy Scripture*. London: Hodder & Stoughton, 1908.

Packer, J. I. *Knowing God*. Downers Grove, Ill.: InterVarsity Press, 1973.

Parker, Joseph. *Preaching Through the Bible*. Grand Rapids, Mich.: Baker Books, 1960.

Pentecost, Dwight. *Will Man Survive?* Chicago: Moody Press, 1971.

Scroggie, Graham, cited by Geoffrey King, *Daniel, A Detailed Explanation of the Book*. London: Henry E. Walter, 1966.

Seiss, Joseph A. *Voices from Babylon*. Philadelphia: Castle Press, 1879.

Tan, Paul Lee, comp. *Encyclopedia of 7700 Illustrations*. Rockville, Md.: Assurance Publishers, 1979.

Tyler, Alexander. Decline and Fall of the Athenian Republic, 1748–1813. N.p., n.d.

Unger, Merrill F. *Biblical Demonology*. Wheaton, Ill.: Van Kampen Press, 1952.

Walvoord, John. *Daniel, Key to Prophetic Revelation*. Chicago: Moody Press, 1971.

ABOUT THE AUTHOR

DAVID JEREMIAH is the founder of Turning Point, an international ministry committed to providing Christians with sound Bible teaching through radio and television, the Internet, live events, and resource materials and books. He is the author of more than fifty books, including *A Life Beyond Amazing, Is This the End?, The Spiritual Warfare Answer Book, David Jeremiah Morning and Evening Devotions, Airship Genesis Kids Study Bible,* and *The Jeremiah Study Bible.*

Dr. Jeremiah serves as the senior pastor of Shadow Mountain Community Church in San Diego, California, where he resides with his wife, Donna. They have four grown children and twelve grandchildren.

Stay connected to the teaching ministry of

DAVID JEREMIAH

Publishing | Radio | Television | Online

Take advantage of three great ways to let Dr. David Jeremiah give you spiritual direction every day!

Turning Points Magazine and Devotional

Receive Dr. Jeremiah's magazine, *Turning Points*, each month:
- Thematic study focus
- 48 pages of life-changing reading
- Relevant articles
- Daily devotional readings and more!

Request *Turning Points* magazine today!
(800) 947-1993 | DavidJeremiah.org/Magazine

Daily Turning Point E-Devotional

Receive a daily e-devotion from Dr. Jeremiah that will strengthen your walk with God and encourage you to live the authentic Christian life.

Sign up for your free e-devotional today!
www.DavidJeremiah.org/Devo

Turning Point Mobile App

Access Dr. Jeremiah's video teachings, audio sermons, and more . . . whenever and wherever you are!

Download your free app today!
www.DavidJeremiah.org/App

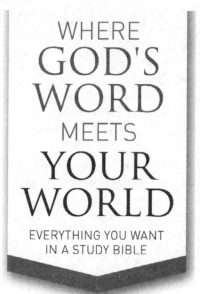

MORE RESOURCES FROM DR. JEREMIAH

• • • • • • • •

Everything You Need

God never intended for us to stumble our way through the course of each day and journey into our future unprepared. He has given us everything we need to walk confidently through life! In *Everything You Need: 8 Essential Steps to a Life of Confidence in the Promises of God*, Dr. Jeremiah examines the words of 2 Peter 1 and shows us how to add diligence, virtue, knowledge, self-control, perseverance, godliness, brotherly kindness, and love to our faith.

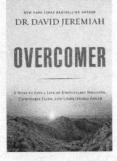

Overcomer

In *Overcomer: Eight Ways to Live a Life of Unstoppable Strength, Unmovable Faith, and Unbelievable Power*, Dr. David Jeremiah explores Paul's description of spiritual armor, explaining what it means for Christians to overcome in this world filled with sin and evil. He explains how, when you put on Christ, you are victorious. You can stand firm against the schemes and strategies of Satan with spiritual armor, and not just stand—but overcome!

The Book of Signs

The Book of Signs will increase your understanding of prophecy and the End Times as Dr. Jeremiah explains 31 signs of the coming Apocalypse. Scripture contains multiple prophecies about the end of the age, and *The Book of Signs* will help you gain greater insight into many of these prophecies, so you can be prepared and guide others to the truths found in the Bible.